SEEING
AS
YOUR
SHOES
ARE
SOON
TO BE
ON
FIRE

LIZA MONROY

SEEING AS YOUR SHOES ARE SOON TO BE ON FIRE

ESSAYS

SOFT SKULL PRESS
BERKELEY

Library of Congress Cataloging-in-Publication Data is available
ISBN 978-1-59376-649-8

Cover design by Jennifer Heuer
Interior design by Megan Jones Design

SOFT SKULL PRESS
An imprint of Counterpoint
2560 Ninth Street, Suite 318
Berkeley, CA 94710
www.softskull.com

Printed in the United States of America
Distributed by Publishers Group West

10 9 8 7 6 5 4 3 2 1

For all the mothers and daughters

CONTENTS

When I was a child, it was clear to me that life was not worth living if we did not know love.

—bell hooks

Nothing is a bigger burden on children than the unlived life of the parent.

—Carl Jung

THE PROFILER'S DAUGHTER

WHEN I WAS fifteen, my mother got my boyfriend deported.

It's like the famous Tolstoy quote about families: every laid-back mother is the same, but every controlling one is controlling in her own special way.

"I'm a profiler,"[1] she is fond of saying. "It's what I do for a living."

In assignments at U.S. consulates and embassies around the world, part of her job entailed deciding whether applicants were qualified for a visa to enter the United States. Were they legitimate students, travelers, or businesspeople? Or were they lying, seeking to enter the country to work illegally? She sat at a counter in an open office in the 1980s, meeting applicants. After terrorism became a concern, she sat behind bulletproof glass, asking questions into a microphone. Visa interviews entailed a series of tests designed to allow her to quickly deduce whether applicants really were who they said they were. Could the surgeon describe equipment used in the operation? Could the chef break down the recipe and equipment used to make his special cannelloni? Could the car repairman explain how a carburetor works?

Every day she caught people trying to trick her.

"I see you're applying for a 'P-3' performers' visa to sing opera in Miami?"

"Yes ma'am."

"Interesting. Where did you study music?"

"In . . . my school. And the opera house in my town."

---

1 See Appendix A: The Profiler Checklist for a complete breakdown.

"I see. Can you demonstrate an aria, please?"

"But I am not warmed up!"

"Do your best."

(Cue off-key Gloria Estefan impersonation.)

With that, her hunch was confirmed, and down came the big red REJECTED stamp. The opera singer turned out to be a cleaning woman working on Albanian trains.

So little in your savings account? REJECTED. Employment: taxi driver? REJECTED. And pre–bulletproof glass, "You're not a bank teller, sir. I smell sheep. You are a sheepherder in Michoacán. But you should know you *can* qualify for an H-2 visa under a special program for agricultural workers."

She preferred stamping APPROVED on applicants' paperwork. Though she and I empathized with people trying to make it to the United States for a better life at any cost, the consistent attempts at deceit brought out her suspicious, mistrustful nature. And I, her teenage daughter, certainly wasn't helping.

This mistrust, along with her outsize tendency to worry, spread to my love life as soon as I was old enough to have one. She evaluated and rapidly assessed the suitability of my suitors, an effort eventually culminating in a "diplomatchmaker" side project that hit its frantic peak in my early thirties. Standing amid the wreckage of another failed serious relationship that had seemed promising at the outset, I turned agency over my romantic pursuits to her. But I trace her habit of applying her job skills to my love life back to my teenage years, given that I was choosing the wrong men even when they were boys.

My petite, charismatic mother was a driven achiever in her youth. She went to Stanford and learned to speak six languages. In 1974, on her way to study in a PhD program in languages in Florence, she met my father, the maître d' on a transatlantic ship. They married after three months together and moved to Seattle, my mother's hometown. I came along five years later, and she became, briefly, a Full-Time Power Mom. But travel and professional ambition called again when Foreign Service recruiters came through Seattle seeking more women applicants. My mother took the exam and, against the odds, she passed.

Our small family—she, my Italian father, and I, a scrap of a girl at four—moved to Washington, D.C., for her three months of training. Her first assignment took us to Guadalajara, Mexico, where she became known for having conducted the most visa interviews in a day. By evening, she chatted up local dignitaries at cocktail parties for Mexican government officials and other international diplomats. She easily disarmed people and got them to open up with her chatty, vivacious nature. Later, I'd wonder if her visa chief job was a cover. The Profiler would've made an excellent spy.

A YEAR INTO this new life, my parents divorced. I suspect they were more in love with each other's passport countries than each other. My father, permanent green card in hand, returned to Seattle. I followed my mother to her subsequent posts—D.C. again, then Rome.

Over spring break when I was nine, our first year in Rome, we traveled to New York to visit my great-uncles, a couple who lived in a loft in Chelsea. My mother took me to see the Woody Allen movie *New York Stories*. One of the segments, "Oedipus Wrecks," is about a man whose mother is so annoying he wishes she would disappear. She does, only to reappear, looming large in the sky over Manhattan, observing and commenting on her son's every move. On the street outside the theater my mother said, "If you're ever tempted to do anything you shouldn't, just remember—that's me, The Big Mom In The Sky."

THREE YEARS INTO her Rome tour, in 1992, Mount Etna erupted. Since being my mother's daughter meant participating in adventure tourism, we packed our weekend bags as if off to the beach.

But one cannot simply walk up an erupting volcano. Military barricades surrounded Mount Etna's base. Ever a problem-solver, The Profiler convinced a curly gray-haired newscaster to transport us in his helicopter to where the rocky lava tumbled into farmlands. The newscaster delivered his report on Italian TV, interviewing devastated farmers. I walked the perimeter of a destroyed farm, black lava rocks hot beneath the rubber soles of my white Keds. As night fell, the alien terrain glowed red behind the newscaster, sweat glistening on his brow from the heat and bright camera lights. My mother had a spark in her eye for him. They spoke animatedly in Italian on the helicopter ride back to the bottom of Mount Etna. Numbers were exchanged, but as with many of her romantic interests, nothing panned out. Love was beyond the realm of anyone's control, even hers. At work, though, The Profiler always nailed it.

When we moved from Rome to Mexico City the following year, the country was in economic and political turmoil. The peso decreased in value from three to a dollar to twelve. Colosio, the ruling PRI party's presidential candidate, was gunned down in Tijuana while giving a speech. In pop culture, the rise of the grunge era meant I no longer had to point to a map to explain to my international classmates where I was born—Seattle was firmly on it.

The Profiler's cases continued.

"You're applying for a tourist visa to go to Disneyland?"

"Si señora."

"Para seis meses?" Six whole months?

"Si señora."

"Pero que va a hacer para seis meses en Disneylandia?" What are you going to do in Disneyland for six months?

"Quiero visitar a Mickey."

REJECTED.

AT FOURTEEN, THE intensity of our single mother/only daughter relationship was suffocating. Her well-intentioned attempts at steering me toward social and scholarly success only helped fuel my rebellion. Though she was one of the smartest and most accomplished people I knew, she was a mother who patrolled my appearance and achievements as if I were a second self. Among the catalogue of things she micromomaged were:

- Clothing. "Wear tropical colors! Everyone in Mexico City will be."

- Hair. It would have met her tropical-colors decree at times, but these were unacceptable palettes for above the neck, resulting in:

  - "Don't dye it that awful shade of whatever."

  - "It's Manic Panic Vampire's Kiss, Mom!"

- Academics. Her gift for math was not genetically passed down to me—algebra was hieroglyphics. Though I did appreciate her poring through research on Malta's Law of the Sea for my Model UN position paper. And, above all else—

- Boys. (Everything that follows.)

At least the tropical-colors advice was wrong. My high school in Mexico City was more New York Fashion Week than Chiquita Banana Lady. My classmates were mostly members of Mexico's elite, daughters and sons of men who ran the country and women who graced the society pages of newspapers. It was *Gossip Girl* south of the border, lifted from scenes from the movie *Y Tu Mamá También*: Busy parents employed maids, drivers, and bodyguards. In a power reversal, the label-clad teens told these adults what to do. The girls wore heels that could take out an eye. Getting a nose job was a de rigueur summer vacation activity. The drinking age was eighteen. Most seniors were legal drinkers anyway, but the funny-because-it's-true joke was that if you're tall enough to see over the bar, you're old enough to order.

I didn't have a driver or bodyguard. I wasn't rich, skinny, or pretty enough to hang with the *fresas* (strawberries), as the it-crowd was called. Instead I hopped taxis and *peseros*—little buses that cost one peso to ride—and invented a lot of fiction about my whereabouts to get a caviar-spoon-sized taste of their lifestyle, too. Nightclubs opened at eleven and went until after sunrise. No one checked ID. On some weeknights the student council members organized *cocteles* (cocktail parties) though such festivities were outside the realm of school-condoned activities.

High school kids going to dressy weeknight cocktail parties sounds ridiculous to me now, the stuff of YA novels with those murderous pointy shoes on their covers. But there it was just the culture, and to us teenagers, the epitome of glamour.

It was also oddly safe and controlled. Who better to keep teens out of trouble than a hired bodyguard standing in the corner by the bar, sipping a Modelo as he peered around the room? The Mexican teens were too sophisticated for ridiculous behavior, anyway. Getting wasted and vomiting into the plants was *so gringo*. I kept myself in check. But two months after arriving, two weeks shy of fourteen, I lost my virginity too soon, to a boy I barely knew, on a whim at a parents-out-of-town house party. My mother found out while reading my diary. Of course she had discovered its secret hiding place. One morning while I was getting ready for school, she cornered me.

"How could you give yourself away to some boy who just wants to use you?" she shouted. "Sex is for adults in loving, committed relationships. Didn't I teach you that?" Tears streamed down her cheeks, provoking my own.

I'd been slut-shamed by my own mother. Doubly humiliated since the boy was also telling everyone at school, rapidly securing me a reputation as "the slut," I escaped into margaritas and Marlboro Lights. The harder my mother worked to rein me in, the wilder I became. I stayed out, going to bars and late-night taquerias. One morning my mother burst out of the front gate in her red bathrobe to catch my friends dropping me off at dawn.

"You all said you were at one another's houses!" she shouted. "I called everyone. ALL THE MOTHERS KNOW!"

The teenage me was so humiliated in front of my friends, who went on to tease me relentlessly. They mussed their hair and shouted, "ALL THE MOTHERS KNOW!" their voices an octave higher than normal.

Getting caught in a lie once didn't stop me from faking a robbery in our own home. My friends and I were smoking weed in a park. A motorcycle cop caught us. He wanted money, a lot of money. Otherwise, it was off to Mexican jail. The rule was guilty until proven innocent, and there was no way even my mother could get us out. She brought *Time* magazine and Cool Ranch Doritos from the embassy commissary to U.S. citizen prisoners. That was the extent of her power when it came to Mexican jail. This was my first brush with true danger. We needed cash, fast.

The only source was the "emergency stash" in the secret compartment of my mother's desk. The cop let one friend and me go to the house to get it while he held the others at the park. High and paranoid, we wondered what we could say to my mother, who was at work, about why this thousand-dollar emergency stash was gone.

"I know!" I said. "Make it look like robbers did it."

We overturned furniture and scattered things. Finished, it looked like a crime scene to me. We returned to the park, paid the cop, and got our friends back. All was well.

When I returned to the house, my mother was home.

"Where's the money?" she asked, her voice as calm and flat as a glassy lake.

Act shocked.

"Oh my god, have we been robbed?"

"Yes. Yes we've been robbed."

"Oh no!"

"By criminals who didn't touch the TV, or stereo, or jewelry, and who just so happened to know about the hidden drawer in my desk."

Poor Profiler. Of course I couldn't pull one over on the spy. Mostly I was just a terrible liar. I ended up apologizing most especially for insulting her intelligence and skills.

She got me back, though.

I MET JEREMY, a sixteen-year-old dropout, through a girl who was dating his friend. A Kurt Cobain lookalike with long blond hair and alien blue eyes, Jeremy spent his days in his room composing songs on his guitar and painting. He reminded me of the Beat Generation figures I was reading about for my English class research paper. Jeremy's room was up a flight of stairs on the top floor of his family's house in the city's posh Polanco district, as if it were a separate apartment, probably intended as a maid's quarters. The room opened out onto a roof deck overlooking the Canadian Embassy.

Jeremy's "apartment" combined with his freedom created an alluring air of independent adulthood. He was a lapsed Mormon who had somehow convinced his parents, probably through his not-very-Mormon life choices, to disown him. He did as he pleased, coming and going at whim. I never saw his parents.

He invited me to hang out with him after school. To get to his house, I started taking the little green and yellow VW Beetle taxis that roamed Mexico City's streets. My new friend would be sitting on the edge of his bed, tucked over his acoustic guitar, strumming a song that sounded like an outtake from the *Nirvana Unplugged* CD we listened to on repeat. He'd show me a painting he'd made earlier that day, lily pads or something oddly Monet-like—soft for a boy who was all rough edges and sharp angles. We kissed a lot that first day, then we were always kissing. Though I would have been willing, we never came close to having sex. I guessed because of ingrained Mormonism, despite his contrarian nature.

His father worked at the U.S. Embassy, too, but in a different area than my mother. The spies had their outpost on The Sixth Floor, where unlike in the rest of the embassy's open floor plan, you needed a code to get in. While the lower floors were bustling with activity, colleagues socializing, and members of the public coming in, The Sixth Floor was silent. My mother attended meetings there sometimes. I still thought more was going on than she let on. In Mexico, she'd also been handling crime show–worthy cases in which she recovered stolen U.S. property—private jets, helicopters, motor homes—from *narcotraficantes* and corrupt government officials. She dealt with death on a near-daily basis: Americans who'd leapt from or been pushed off hotel balconies, who'd been murdered, or who'd accidentally been beaten to death in robberies. Not even becoming an obstinate teenager could stop her stories from impressing me. Her office wall was plastered with thank-you notes and photographs of her standing in front of the recovered property, and others alongside various presidents, foreign heads of state (even anti-American Hugo Chavez of Venezuela), and the occasional international celebrity headed to the U.S. on an O-1 "exceptional talent" visa to shoot a movie or perform a concert. My mother was a hero to many. I just didn't want her to be my hero. I wasn't lost property that needed recovery. My fifteen-year-old self didn't want her APPROVED stamp.

"I'm not a spy," my mother always said. Only a spy could be so good at denying her status as a spy while simultaneously displaying such excellence at spying. Nothing slipped past The Profiler. So when I'd cut school to spend a whole day with Jeremy, she found out.

"I didn't know where you were," she said, though I was certain this was bait. Spy bait. She always knew where I was.

"I was just over at—"

"That boy's house. When you were supposed to be at school. You're not to see him again."

Of course, telling a teenager she can't do something is merely an invitation for her to further pursue that very thing in a more clandestine way.

One Saturday night, Jeremy mentioned he had microdots, and did I want to take one? I'd smoked pot and shot tequila but knew nothing about any other mind-altering substances. He placed a small white paper ball on my tongue. I let it sit for a while before I swallowed.

Forty minutes passed. We were on the subway when a feverish feeling surged in my stomach. The sound of the train on the tracks morphed into a drumbeat. I heard the rhythm of the entire universe. We got off the train in the touristy Zona Rosa near the embassy. From the outside, we must have looked like any teen boyfriend and girlfriend, walking around on a weekend night holding hands. No one could see my brain splitting open.

I gaped at all the shapes and colors and movements. Mexico City was magical, and Jeremy was some kind of strange foreign Beat-grunge prophet walking its streets, all tall and long with that sheet of golden hair. We sat down beside the *Angel de la Independencia* statue, the shiny angel of gold sitting high in the middle of a traffic circle on Paseo de la Reforma. I watched as her wings began to flap, at first slowly, then with increasing speed the more focused I became, until she rose off her pillar and took off into the night sky. It was my first and only true hallucination, not counting later ones I'd have about certain men.

"Did you see—" I said to Jeremy, but when I glanced back at the pillar there she was, a statue just like before. "She flew away, but she came back."

I didn't learn until later, when I looked it up on the brand-new dial-up World Wide Web that was already stocked with drug information, that microdots were tiny LSD capsules, and what I'd had was an acid trip.

I continued seeing Jeremy as often as I could sneak away. We didn't repeat our microdot adventure. Our mainly mundane teenage afternoons were spent painting and listening to music in his room. He taught me some guitar. We smoked basic Mexican pot. My grades were decent, except of course for algebra, and I figured I wasn't giving my mother any cause for suspicion.

Then one day he was gone. Just gone. On the phone, the housekeeper would only say he was no longer there.

"Cuando va a regresar?" I asked. When is he coming back?

"No señorita. El Jeremy ya no regresa mas."

Not coming back, EVER? What happened? Why would he leave without telling me? I didn't know what to do. I called friends, went to his neighborhood, walked past his house. I wandered home wondering, *Where did you go?* In my room, I played the *Nirvana Unplugged* CD and cried. The mystery lasted until that evening, when my mother got home from work.

"The DEA have deported Jeremy," she said. "And they know about you, too."

"What do you mean, they 'know about me'?"

"They knew he was taking drugs. They searched his room and came over here, too, and found a water bottle that you converted into a pipe for smoking marijuana. In your closet. They've taken it as evidence. They've been watching you from the roof of the Canadian Embassy. He was returned to the States to be charged, and unless this behavior ends you'll be following shortly."

AN UNUSUAL FATE had befallen my dear teenage American boyfriend: deportation from Mexico back to the U.S. I cried and worried about being arrested, but it turned out I was only grounded. I wondered why Jeremy got it so much worse.

"Can you believe the DEA had Jeremy deported?" I said to a friend at school. "What if they're coming after me next?"

Sometimes all it takes is a pair of outside ears to allow you to hear your own naïveté.

"Dude," my friend said. "The DEA can't deport someone from another country. And even if they could, they kinda have more important stuff to do in Mexico than bust a couple of American teenagers for smoking weed."

The reality became glaringly obvious, so close I hadn't seen it.

"Oh shit. It was my mom."

"It was totally your mom! Your mom is crazy."

It had become a personal mission to get rid of the bad boy who captured her daughter's affections. I was still her favorite case. Like me, she was a terrible liar, and I was particularly gullible.

"You got Jeremy sent away!" I blurted when she came home from work.

She didn't deny it.

"He was a bad influence. He's better off somewhere else, where he can't give drugs to my daughter."

She confessed to hiding in a car outside his house or visiting a friend at the Canadian Embassy, waiting to see if I would come out.

"You followed me?"

"I didn't know where you were," she repeated.

"Where else did you look?"

She shrugged. "Pasta caprese sound good for dinner?"

I shouldn't have been surprised. The Profiler was always looking out. Why did she do it? Intense love, concern, her need for control, fear of losing her only child, her baby girl . . . there were many reasons, but she wouldn't give me any specific, concrete answer because I suspect she didn't have one.

As I got older, my mother revealed more about her own past. She shared stories about her time at Stanford, baking her own pot brownies and going to see Country Joe and the Fish at the Fillmore, a San Francisco venue that had the first light shows. "We smoked pot and ate baklava," she said. "Honey dripped all over my nice suede jacket." I wondered when and how she'd become so stringent.

"You were rebellious and impossible," she said. "And in high school—running around and being difficult."

WITH THE ADVENT of the internet, her 1989 Big Mom In The Sky prophecy—or was it a threat?—became eerily possible. While she couldn't literally watch from the sky, when it came to her profiling my romantic choices, she could spy from afar, thanks to Google and Facebook. By then I'd moved back to the States, to college in Boston and a couple of years in film industry jobs in Los Angeles until, at twenty-three, I landed in New York City. Even when The Profiler could no longer deport the men I chose to date, she continued to spy remotely from Italy, Venezuela, and Spain, wielding her proverbial REJECTED stamp.

"That one doesn't even have a savings account."

REJECTED.

"I don't like what he posts on Facebook."

REJECTED

"He's not a bad person. He's just not right for you."

REJECTED

She signed her emails,

Momager

Trust But Verify

Can someone (The Profiler) or something (a computer algorithm) weed out who's wrong for you? I didn't think so. Which made it even more annoying that she was right.

A note from the desk of

THE PROFILER

I NEVER IMAGINED that my diplomatic career in the State Department Foreign Service would provide me with the right "tool set" to become Profiler Mom. Like it or not, romance, love, and finding that "perfect partner" are a challenge for most of us. And we do make mistakes. Many. What better way to help my daughter zero in on promising suitors—and discard the dicey ones—than by "profiling" the boys—later men—she chose to date? Sounds good, right? She didn't think so.

What is profiling? Consciously and unconsciously, we form first impressions of people we see or meet each day. How? By observing their physical appearance, verbal and nonverbal communication, interactions, and other cues.

Deciding whether visa applicants and Americans seeking U.S. passports or funds qualified was easier than finding Mr. Right. I had years of experience dealing with a diverse public in different countries. Demand for consular services is high; lines are long. Officers question applicants, check documents, and decide within minutes—does he/she qualify?

Was the "musician" in front of me really part of a group scheduled to perform in Las Vegas? Was the "surgeon" traveling to a conference in Chicago a bona fide doctor? What about the veiled woman, supposedly part of an Arabian diplomat's household staff? Appearance: check. Did they "look" right for their occupation? Knowledge: check. Could they answer questions about their work confidently, correctly with no hesitation? Visa: issued or denied.

At the American Citizen Services counter: Did that backpacker really get robbed and have no one to give/send him money? Did another lose his passport again—or maybe sell it to counterfeiters to alter for a foreigner to seek entry to the U.S.? How could that lady in her late fifties give birth with no medical assistance in a tiny Mexican village a week after leaving the U.S.? Yet she claimed the infant at the interview window was her own, natural offspring.

As you follow Liza's (mis)adventures in dating, I'll pop in with suggestions.[2] Now mature (?), Liza has given me creative license to add some thoughts. (Of course she commands the Delete key, so I'm hoping for the best.)

---

2 Disclaimer on the presence of The Profiler's notes throughout the text: *Why would you let your mother write in your book?* you may be wondering. *It's YOUR book. Isn't the point that you wanted to break free of her controlling ways?* Yes and no. Her presence here illustrates my point: she didn't even want me to write this book without putting her official stamp on it. ("I can help!" she said.) But instead of cutting her out, I let her in. We've each improved at accepting—even embracing?—the other as is. Most of the time.

TWO HUSBANDS
REAL AND FAKE

> Many people in my generation are children of true divorce who pre-
> fer to do a pilot run "marriage," raising surrogate babies, such
> as plants and animals, before advancing to a formal agreement
> involving aspirational words and phrases such as "forever" and
> "until death do us part."
>
> —Kassi Underwood, *May Cause Love: An Unexpected Journey of*
> *Enlightenment After Abortion*

IT WAS THE best of marriage, it was the worst of marriage: one was platonic, one was sexual, one was in poverty, one was in riches, one was passionate, one was temperate, one was in the open, one was secret, one was tender, one was hard, one was of equals, one was a power struggle, one was convenient, one was troublesome, one was lasting, one was finite, one was honest, one was deceitful. One was real, one was fake.

Call it a tale of two husbands. And as with any false binary, one of the opposites gained favor over the other before it all got entangled and blown apart.

ONCE UPON A time, or rather five days after my twenty-second birthday, Emir and I drove to Las Vegas, where we were married, naturally, by an Elvis impersonator. We danced our way down the aisle to where he stood, his red jumpsuit flashing under the disco lights.

"Do you promise to always walk your hound dogs and polish each other's blue suede shoes?" he boomed into the mic.

We didn't own hound dogs or blue suede shoes, but our vow to love each other until death wasn't a real lie.

THE DAY EMIR walked into our film production class at our college in Boston, I stared across the room at him, seated at one of those old-school chairs with a desk attached, taking off his hat and adjusting his dark hair. I couldn't figure out why I recognized him though we'd never met before. He resembled someone. It took me the better part of two hours to realize that "someone" was me. Dark and petite with olive skin and an easy smile, he could have been my long-lost fraternal twin. I'm Jewish and Italian but frequently mistaken for Iranian, Lebanese, or Turkish. Our resemblance might have made Emir and me notice each other—what is more interesting than encountering ourselves?—but soon, while working on our student film, an adaptation of the William S. Burroughs short story "The Junky's Christmas," we realized we were similar beneath the surface, too: both of us, as Emir put it, were "love-fools." He had recently come out of the closet and had had his heart swiftly broken. He thought he'd be with his first love forever.

I was still reeling over mine.

I MET JULIAN the summer before my senior year of high school. He had already graduated and was back in Mexico City, staying at his mother's while interning at a financial firm. A mutual friend introduced us. I was leaning against a tree outside her house, wearing a long black silk skirt, a hand-me-down from my mother.

"Do you know you have snails crawling up your skirt?" he asked. Three snails were winding up the silk, approaching thigh height, leaving rainbow trails in their wake. It's the only thing that's ever happened to me that was lifted from the pages of magical realism. Sixteen-year-old me interpreted this as a sign.

Julian and I were both nomads of sorts, making our homes anywhere and carrying them wherever we went. An Austrian Mexican, Julian was tall and attractive in a Viking sort of way, with deep green eyes. We'd each lived in three countries and held two passports.

He came over the next night in a suit, toting a bottle of amaretto. In high school, I loved this sickly-sweet liqueur. My mother often spent the night at her then-boyfriend Harvey's house after putting in long days at the embassy. I thought it was cool that she trusted me, though I have no idea why she did. She picked me up every morning for my clerical job in the visa section and dropped me off when our workdays ended at five, continuing on to Harvey's. I knew this man wasn't right for my mom, but I appreciated him because their relationship left my evenings free and deflected her attention from me.

During those free evenings, I took meandering walks around Mexico City with Julian. I loved his stories. He called himself The Coca-Cola Baby because when he was born early he weighed the same as a two-liter Coke bottle. In fourth grade, he fell three stories onto concrete. Despite all odds, not only did he survive, he avoided any damage to his razor-sharp intellect. He was hospitalized for months but came back even stronger. He lived in Europe and Mexico with his mother, a grand, bottle-blond diva with pink lipstick and turquoise eye shadow that matched her eyes, who struggled with mental illness. When she moved Julian back to Mexico for his high school years, they spent a year living in a hotel. He'd loved living in the hotel, he said, how clean it always was and the meals delivered at the press of a button, but longed for a feeling of home. Eventually they moved into an apartment. Julian graduated salutatorian of his class, going on a full ride to an Ivy League university. It was easy to see why. He was sharp and funny, and I was in awe of him. When we kissed on my plaid flannel bedspread, drunk on amaretto and, for me, the smell of his Eternity for Men cologne, I had a hunch that here was the person I was going to marry. Underneath his suits were tattoos he designed himself. He was a math whiz and a talented artist. He was everything, I thought. *BOOM—soul mate found at age sixteen—won at life!*

We went out for all-you-can-eat tacos and competed to see who could eat the most. Usually, I won. We stumbled home laughing that a petite, five-foot-two girl could out-taco a hefty Bavarian man. In my room at night, in a house where we could be alone, we shyly undressed each other under the flannel bedspread in the dark. Neither of us was especially experienced when it came to sex, but we made up for it in sheer chemistry. He had a mass of chest hair he called "the carpet," and afterward I snuggled in, feeling as if I didn't need anything else.

My mother actually liked Julian. He fit her textbook profile. International background. Ivy League education. Cosmopolitan. Spoke three languages. Ambitious. Even then she predicted he'd be successful. He talked economics and current events with her. He was a big man with big plans.

Plans that involved, at summer's end, returning to his economics classes, preparing for a Wall Street life. We fell out of touch for a while, but not a day went by that I didn't pine. I played my Breeders and Smashing Pumpkins CDs, teaching myself bass lines while sitting on my flannel bedspread, wistfully looking out the window and remembering nights Julian walked through the gate down below, toting amaretto and flowers. He was the first person I wrote to when I opened an email account the following spring. He replied mentioning a girlfriend. I would make myself okay with being his friend, but in the depths of my soulplace I was certain Julian was the one. The problem was I often mistook the extreme willpower that drove me to make things happen for the magic of fate.

THREE YEARS passed.

MY THIRD YEAR of college, Julian visited me in Boston. He was single again, working at his first Wall Street job. Over red wine and pasta *fatta in casa* in the North End, it seemed we'd never been apart. A few months later, he gave me my first cell phone, on a plan linked to his, our numbers one digit apart. His generosity and sweeping romantic gestures made me feel invincible. Though I was headed to L.A. for an internship in the fall, along with Emir, who had become a close friend, Julian and I made plans: after I graduated in December, I would move to New York to live with him, marry him.

HE FLEW TO L.A. on weekends. At a diner in Hollywood late at night, Julian gave me a chocolate box filled with painted snail shells. The metaphor had become one of "our things" since the snails on my skirt the night we met: we were slow to come back to each other, too. Each shell contained a rolled piece of paper, fortune cookie–length reasons why he loved me. The final shell was the largest. I suspected it contained a ring. I held it a little longer than the others. I tried to conceal my disappointment when I reached in and pulled out another piece of paper. I wouldn't stay disappointed for long, anyway. Julian was just trying to throw me off. The ring sat on my finger when I woke up the next morning. He'd slipped it on in my sleep. Romantic or creepy? At the time it didn't cross my mind to think of it as anything but the former. I gazed in awe at the stone. An oblong diamond. Marquise, he said. For someone obsessed with marriage, I knew little about wedding rituals: ring shapes, dress styles, flower arrangements. All that had little to do with my fantasy, which consisted entirely of an idealized vision of domesticity.

IT MIGHT BE more compelling if I'd lost my tragic-figure fiancé in some catastrophic way, but it was the more mundane condition most commonly known as cold feet. The feet in question belonged to me, or so I thought. I called him, fishing for reassurance two weeks before I was supposed to move to New York.

"I'm nervous," I said.

"Maybe you should just stay in L.A. then," he answered abruptly.

Here was the "other" Julian, the one who disappeared for days without explanation that summer we were first together and resurfaced to no questions. I was devastated. I threatened to drive right off Mulholland if he really left me. It wasn't just that we were too young for what we thought we wanted. Instability raised us both: absent alcoholic fathers; intense single mothers; and us, their epiphyte children. His retreat made me clingy and crazy. There was romance in that sense of doom, a reason the most famous love stories are tragedies. *Every happy couple is alike.*

I missed him so much I lost control, emailing and calling incessantly until he told me to stop. Had all those reasons on those slips of paper been a lie? I toted the ring to a few pawnshops but my conscience wouldn't let me go through with it, and I sent it back to his secretary via certified mail. The only thing that came back to me was half a green receipt slip.

IN AUGUST OF 2001, I flew to New York by myself in an attempt to get him back. It would be different if we saw each other in person, I told myself. I had a backup plan to stay with a friend in case it turned out to be a disaster. I stood at the pay phone outside Julian's office (he'd taken the cell phone away), fresh off a red-eye in the muggy afternoon, nine months after we'd broken our engagement. We had barely spoken, but I showed up unannounced to tell him we really did belong together and I was moving to New York City to prove it. It was the kind of thing only stalkers, *Sex and the City* characters, or early-twentysomethings would do. I was at least one of those things.

He came downstairs, informed me that I was crazy, and said that he was leaving on a business trip to Colombia in the morning.

"Inspecting a pipeline," he said. "In a jungle with gorillas. Could be dangerous."

"Gorillas?"

"*Guerrillas.*" He smiled. "You look good."

We met later near his apartment on 86th and York. He was walking an orange cat on a leash. This was typical of eccentric Julian. One of the things I loved most about him was that he consistently surprised me and defied expectations: a Wall Street power broker leash-training a little cat he adored. We ascended to his studio—all pizza boxes, analyst reports, and overflowing trashcans—and dropped off the cat. At the bar downstairs, he listened to my speech about why breaking things off was a mistake.

"If you move here," he said, "we can see."

From a friend's East Village rooftop a few nights later, the Twin Towers loomed above. I stared, almost praying as if they were representations of deities at an altar, *Make my life in New York as sparkling and magical as you.*

IN LOS ANGELES a couple of weeks later, in September of 2001, I only became more determined.

"Don't do it," my mother said as September turned to October and my plans for a move to New York developed anyway. "There's anthrax there. The whole city's a mess."

But nothing would stop me. Not anthrax, orange-level terrorism alerts, or my mother.

MEANWHILE, EMIR HAD been seeking an employer to sponsor him for a work visa so he could stay in the country legally. But after the terrorist attacks and with the economy on a downswing, no Hollywood production companies were hiring, or at least not sponsoring immigrants for the "unskilled labor" of assistant positions. It wasn't worth the bureaucracy and paperwork required to obtain an H1B work visa for an employee. Instead, Emir served pasta at a Sunset Strip restaurant and wrote screenplays that placed as finalists in national competitions. None of this would lead to a legitimate means by which to stay. As a young man from a Middle Eastern country in post–September 11 America, finding a job was impossible. Time (on his student visa) was running out. There were no more options.

On Halloween night in West Hollywood, I dropped to one knee at our favorite gay bar.

"I'll marry you," I said.

Suddenly it seemed as if there was a reason I hadn't married Julian.

I always say that talking with me about immigration is like asking a mechanic's daughter about engines. I grew up around visas, those laminated welcome passes to the United States. My mother spent part of her twenty-six-year career in the State Department as a visa chief. My first summer job was slipping the glossy admittance cards back into passports in the consular section of the U.S. Embassy in Mexico where she was stationed. Since I understood the system, I knew that the best way to help my bestie was through marriage. (Rebelling against my mother was another specialty of mine, but I would have asked Emir to marry me even if it wouldn't have upset my mother.) Helping Emir would be easy because it was the opposite of what I'd always wanted. It might even be free therapy, freeing me of my intense fear of divorce by making it inevitable, and it would be a happy divorce at that, because it would mean he got his green card. This marriage, I told myself, would not bring heartbreak, because it wasn't real. There was no passion involved, no heated attachment of the kind that came with sexual love.

EMIR AND I got married by that Elvis impersonator and moved to New York together. We arrived in April and shared a tiny fifth-floor walkup on the Lower East Side. Orchard Street was still all leather shops, and you had to cross Houston into the East Village to go to a restaurant. I worked in publishing, and Emir found a job as an office manager at a softcore gay bodybuilder porn company in Chelsea and kept writing screenplays.

An email from Julian arrived. He'd nearly died in a surfing accident in Mexico. When he was in the hospital, he wrote, he couldn't stop thinking of me.

That was all it took. If he was back in, so was I. We met at the Gramercy Hotel bar for cocktails and so he could lend his expertise to the 401(k) options that had just become available to me in my entry-level position in publishing. Not wanting to disturb how well our reunion drink was going, I didn't mention Emir as anyone more than my roommate.

Julian and I were back together for a few months when he started acting distant again, and I discovered his feelings for a coworker when I found a card he'd written her on a long weekend we'd taken together, saying he wished she was there, not mentioning me. I packed up the clothes I'd stashed in a drawer in his apartment and took a cab back to the Lower East Side, the lights and swarms of people all along the avenue blurred behind the tears that flowed soundlessly down my cheeks because I was too humiliated to cry in front of the driver. At home, though, with Emir, I lost it. He never said "I told you so." He gave me a hug and listened.

A RELATIONSHIP WITH Julian had failed again, but Emir and I succeeded in our Immigration and Naturalization Service (INS) interview journey, ultimately convincing the officers that our marriage was legitimate. We talked up our domestic disturbances about my lack of dishwashing skills and his smoking.

One night soon after, Emir burst into our apartment out of breath, holding an opened piece of official mail from the INS, color drained from his face.

"Are you okay?" I asked.

"This is unbelievable."

"What happened? Are they investigating us?"

"I won the green card lottery!"

"What? How?"

"I entered every year, just in case."

"Just in case what? I didn't come through?"

"I never imagined I would win."

It wasn't much of a backup plan, but it made sense that he'd have one, and now it had come through despite nearly impossible odds. Of the fifteen million who enter the only immigration program that offers an easy, fast path toward citizenship, just fifty thousand random lucky ones are drawn from the hat each year.

As if fate were playing a Shakespearean joke, Emir got his green card on his own, without any help from me. He'd gone from no means by which to stay to two options: the marriage or the lottery. He chose the lottery, since it required no fakery. Still, we didn't divorce. There was no real reason to. Our marriage worked. Why bother with all that paperwork?

THAT WINTER, I was promoted to assist a literary agent. And Julian, as he tended to do, reappeared. Neither of us mentioned the other woman. It was as if she never existed. That felt so long ago, anyway. It would be different this time. After exchanging emails for a couple of weeks, in which I mentioned how cold it was, Julian sent back confirmation for two tickets to Puerto Rico for the weekend, in his name and mine. Sweeping grand gestures—and surprise trips—were my weakness.

As the city warmed, Julian took me to a romantic dinner in the Meatpacking District. It seemed as if something was amiss, and I wondered, again, if he was going to propose. My heart beat faster every time he reached for the bread knife. But nothing. When the check came, I hoped my disappointment wasn't obvious. He slept over, and when I woke, a new diamond ring, even bigger than the last, rested on my finger. As with the first time, my yes was a given.

I didn't think about implied consent then. Immature and naïve, I was blinded by love for our story. What were the chances of someone who moved to different countries every few years ending up with her high school sweetheart? I was going to get married! But first I had to get divorced. I was engaged while still married. I had to tell Julian about Emir. I'd kept it a secret for so long, I was a little bit terrified of Julian's reaction.

I asked him to meet me at a crowded Midtown bar after work. Telling him felt like telling my mother—I was cowering and hesitant, guilty, as I perceived myself through their eyes, of audacious and possibly criminal behavior—and I was right: Julian was enraged.

"What did he ever do to deserve to stay in this country?" he shouted above the blaring music. I launched into a discussion of my reasons, but Julian's question had been rhetorical.

"He's like your pet," he interrupted. "All he's missing is a tail."

EMIR AND I sat side by side at his desk sharing a big bag of chips and figuring out what rationale to put on our divorce papers. (New York was still a fault state in 2003, making "irreconcilable differences" not an option.) For some reason we wanted this to feel true, even though our marriage hadn't been. We didn't want to claim "adultery," or "mental cruelty." Something so false did not seem fair. We settled on "abandonment," code for lack of sex. A real reason for dissolving a fake marriage. Yet as Emir and I separated in anticipation of my real one, I realized that while our union may have been legally fake, the comfort and security it brought were not.

Married or not, we were a bonded pair for life. I was already nostalgic for our rituals: takeout from the Japanese place downstairs; neighborhood gay bar hopping; watching our shows (*Ab Fab*, *Sex and the City*); and long, late-night talks about our shared ambitions (screenwriting), our mutual pattern of loving guys who never seemed to love us quite as much as we loved them, and family dramas (my mother's control issues, his father's homophobia). There must be no easy divorces. But I told myself it was worth it, because Julian was on the other side. I didn't need him to love me as much as I loved him, as long as I got to be with him.

We moved in together in New York and planned our July wedding ceremony in Mexico. In November, Julian, who was (like Emir) not a U.S. citizen, told me the lawyers at his investment bank had made a paperwork mistake and he might have to work out of the London office until it was resolved.

"We're engaged anyway," I said. "We could just go ahead and get married."

We went to City Hall, another rushed ceremony because of the need for a green card. Emir and a female college friend of Julian's were in attendance. Emir was going to be the witness, but Julian suggested that it might look strange to the INS if the wife's ex-husband who got a green card was the witness in her second wedding to a foreigner who was to get a green card through the marriage. The four of us drank bodega champagne on the sidewalk, and then we went to work. It was 10 AM. It wasn't a dream wedding, but given that I harbored no fantasies about dresses, bouquets, and banquets, the wedding was never my dream anyway. The City Hall wedding was just for Julian's corporate-immigration convenience (though I wasn't sure why he objected to uprooting to London for a while).

We had started planning the "real" wedding, which, as a purely symbolic ceremony, was actually the opposite. Wanting to wed in the country in which we'd met, we would "get married" in Mexico, in July. Julian suggested we get married by a Mayan shaman, just because. The ceremony would be conducted entirely in Mayan, a language we did not speak or understand. Cultural appropriation at its worst, but at the time I didn't question it because I wouldn't question Julian.

Even when it turned out marriage to him came with strings attached.

"It needs to look like the Four Seasons in here when I get home," he said of the small one-bedroom apartment we shared in Manhattan's Chelsea neighborhood.

"You miss living in a hotel?"

He didn't find my nudge at his past funny. After work, he yelled about my piles of books and papers. He wanted to throw them all away.

"But I got your suits from the dry cleaner's!" I was desperate, frantic for his approval.

"That's one thing on the list."

"I'm sorry."

"Don't apologize. Do the tasks."

Marriage can bring out a different side of someone you thought you knew, but you may have to marry them in order to see it. One of my pet names for Julian was Meanball. When his Hyde side came out, I'd call him that. He didn't seem to mind. Ever the optimist, I had tried to turn his meanness into something I could perceive as a cute, unintentional, and minor part of his large personality. My mother knew The Finance Prince, not Meanball. As Meanball spent more and more time hanging around during our marriage, Julian turned into the type of man my mother would have warned me about.

The problem with superficial evaluations is they evaluate the superficial parts of a person. And Julian happened to cut into The Profiler's Achilles' heel with his impressive career, fine suit, and charisma. I hadn't known his definition of marriage meant expectations for me to turn into a 1950s-style homemaker. Cook. Clean. Do the housekeeping. Pick up his suits at the dry cleaner's. It wasn't that I was opposed to doing the domestic. I wanted to share our responsibilities, divide the work of living evenly: rent, housecleaning, and chores. Split the bills. Split the everything. We both worked full-time. I earned less, but there was no way I could even come close, as a writer and editor, to his Wall Street salary. I never considered not working, which he agreed with. He didn't want a housewife who depended on him for financial support, and that wasn't the "marriage genre" I was looking for either. It didn't add up. Julian agreed with the equal-division marriage model when it came to money, but not domestic duties. Either he hadn't shown a chauvinistic side in our pre-marriage life, or I'd had blinders firmly on because I wanted Julian to be Prince Charming.

The old Julian wasn't around as much, the bright, eccentric, hilarious guy I fell in love with as a teenager. There were glimmers that shone when conditions were right, like when he read a memoir set in Vanuatu and spent a few months strategizing about quitting Wall Street so we could move there and lead a simpler life in a house on stilts. He wouldn't obsess about how much of his salary went to city taxes. He wouldn't be paranoid about some impending economic collapse he swore was right around the corner (which it was). Suits and dress shoes would be replaced by board shorts and flip-flops. After his fourteen-hour days at a now-defunct investment bank, we'd lie on the couch while the cat darted around and talk about how wonderful everything would be once we got to Vanuatu.

IN MEXICO, IN July, Emir walked me down the aisle at the "real" wedding. In our white clothes, Julian and I faced forward, toward the turquoise lull of the Caribbean. Sage was burned and blessings recited in Mayan. If you didn't understand a ritual's content, was it real? A thing with sand, a thing with candles. No vows spoken. A tourist in a bikini made a cameo in the photos. Afterward, we were set to stay another five days at the resort, which I had considered our honeymoon. Then I found out Julian had also arranged for his mother to stay extra days, too.

"Your mother is going to be on our honeymoon?" I said in disbelief. "Even my mother is leaving."

"She deserves a nice vacation," he said. "And that's what it is. Honeymoons are stupid. We just spent all this money on the wedding."

Ah, his mother. Hot-pink bikini, long, slender legs, open-toed stilettos revealing perfectly pedicured toes at the hotel pool. Her dyed blond hair was always up in a tight french twist, her makeup flawlessly applied. She was impossible in a different way than my mother was. High maintenance. Classic diva. Julian paid her bills and living expenses. He was her only child with a mad scientist who had ten other children. "She's had a hard life," Julian would say. As a girl she lived in an Austrian town taken over by Nazis. He also once told me she was suspicious of my mother and me, that she'd said of us, "Watch out for those Jews, they will try to take all your money." I was aghast, but already the reels in my head were playing. *He's saying it to get a rise out of me.* Or, *She's mentally unstable, who knows what traumas and horrors have done to her mind . . .*

Had growing up with a parent who was judgmental for a living made me so anti-judgment that as a young person I ended up ignoring or excusing away all kinds of bad behavior—down to chauvinism and anti-Semitism?

When Julian and I did want some alone time on the not-honeymoon, we went scuba diving. The best place to get away from his mother was underwater.

CHRISTMAS EVE OF my twenty-fifth year, I was pregnant. Our contraception had failed. Julian and I had firm plans: we would have kids after I turned thirty. That gave us five years for Julian to be running Wall Street and for Citibank to "open their vaults" for my own questionably forthcoming riches before we would start a family.

"Well, you're married," the doctor said when she gave me the official test result. "And a good age to get started."

I explained that we weren't ready, that this just wasn't in our plans right now, feeling the need to justify it to this doctor, who didn't do "the procedure." I told Julian what she'd said.

"Should we consider . . . ?"

"Make the appointment."

Right. Do the tasks.

"HOW ARE YOU feeling?" Emir asked when we met at a Chelsea wine bar a few nights later.

"I was nauseated all last week. Now I feel a weird connection to animals," I said, staring at a dog outside. Our eyes met, then it lifted its leg to pee on a garbage bag.

"And you're sure about ending it? I don't want you to have any regrets."

I took a gulp of wine.

"So, yes," he said.

"We're not ready."

"Come over after, if you want. I'll get lunch, we can watch some *Ab Fab*."

I RODE THE subway to the clinic alone, blaming hormones for my crying when really it was grief for the state of my marriage, for the pregnancy, for Julian, in his expensive suit, meeting me in the waiting room. He'd had a morning meeting—by then he was one of the youngest managing directors on Wall Street. Seated in a plastic orange chair, he typed messages on his BlackBerry about investments in Latin American energy companies. I didn't consider that maybe we couldn't go through with having this baby because we didn't love each other anymore. If we did, how could we have ended the pregnancy? And how could I have felt so relieved? Only later would I feel conflicted. Not regretful, but a delayed sense of mourning that trickled like a light rain. If I wanted to create the kind of nuclear family I didn't have growing up, here had been the opportunity. It wasn't the right time, we'd said. But can there be a wrong time with the right person?

MY FIRST HUSBAND knew I was struggling in my second marriage, but my first husband, unlike my second husband, was the one I turned to for comfort.

Things continued unspooling. Julian wanted to hire a dwarf performer for a colleague's birthday party.

"That's degrading," I said.

"It's the little dude's job—he *wants* to do it. No once forces him. He gets *paid*."

When I was invited to a writing residency in Orlando for the summer, to spend three months working in Jack Kerouac's former home, Julian forbade me to go.

"You have so many vacation days, though," I said. "We can trade off a few long weekends and see almost as much of each other as we do at home."

"No way," he said. "I need you."

For a moment, I felt one of those glimmers of hope wave upward from the gloom, flashing like a silver fish beneath a shallow surface.

"You need me?" I repeated.

"Who will pick up my suits?"

"YOU HAVE TO go," Emir wrote me in a concerned email. "What's the next thing he's going to tell you that you 'can't' do?" So I went.

In the Kerouac house, on my own for the first time since we'd gotten back together four years earlier, I cried because I missed Julian. But as the days went on and I settled into the quiet space and time of a quaint historic neighborhood in Orlando, it was as if a chain-link veil had lifted. During our next phone call, I sought reassurance as I had six years before from Los Angeles, though this time, we were married. My line of questioning, too, had evolved: "We're still going to have kids when I'm thirty, right?" I asked. "We're still going to be together, right? Live on Vanuatu in a house on stilts?" He said yes, said I was annoying for asking for so much reassurance, but that didn't stop my persistent questions. Sometimes you have to hold on to a person for years to finally figure out that you will never know their true intentions.

Halfway through the summer, Julian flew to Miami for his birthday. I met him there. We went to a big, fancy, boring bottle-service club with his banker colleagues. Back in the hotel room close to dawn, Julian, drunk and raging, tried to throw my laptop across the room. I grabbed my purse, ran to the lobby, and got into a taxi to the airport. I flew back to Orlando stunned by how far gone my marriage was. The morning sun blared in my eyes on the ride from the airport to the house. My ears rang from the deafening music the night before. I was *done*, I told myself over and over, a mantra. *Done done done*. In the late afternoon, Julian showed up on the front porch of Jack Kerouac's house. I stepped outside and closed the door behind me. A breeze rustled the Spanish moss on the big old oak on the front lawn.

"What are you doing here?"

"What happened?" he asked. "I'm so sorry."

He didn't remember any of it, but he promised to quit drinking if I would return to Miami to finish the weekend, which I did.

I'M SURE YOU already know that we never made it to Vanuatu.

AT THE END of August in New Jersey, where we had relocated (Julian's goal was to make money—lots of it—and you didn't have to pay New York City taxes if you lived in New Jersey), I haphazardly packed some suitcases while he was at work. In one afternoon with a U-Haul, I went from Wall Street Wife to first-year graduate student living with three anonymous roommates in an East Village apartment that Emir helped me find. It was a few blocks from his own apartment, the one we lived in together when we first moved to New York. The apartment smelled like weed, and the neighborhood felt like home. When I was twenty-two I moved here with Emir, hoping to reunite with Julian. Five years later, I returned to the same place to be free of him.

JULIAN AND I attended a string of doomed therapy sessions after I moved out.

"Do you realize you have a traumatized wife?" the therapist said. "That you cut her off every time she opens her mouth to speak?"

Was that what I was? Traumatized? Like many who experience emotional abuse, I'd had no idea. I thought the problem was me. The therapist's comments pushed me off the tightrope I was somehow still walking between marriage and divorce. I didn't want to be a divorcée, even though I already was one. Technically at least.

Julian asked me to stay married until his green card was finalized. In exchange, he offered money.

"Don't let me get kicked out of the country," he said.

We entered into precisely the kind of arrangement he once chided me for. Emir never even brought up the issue of compensation, but now I let Julian pay me. After resisting "taking his money" for years, I suddenly had no qualms about it. We'd had a weird transactional aspect to our relationship the whole time. We'd stay married, and I could continue accessing a joint account. I spent the next year in a fake marriage with my real husband. The great marriage was an arrangement of convenience with my gay friend, and the "real" one—with Prince Charming—was a disaster.

ONE OF THE last things Julian said to me was, "No one will ever know you as well as I know you, and you will never find anyone else who loves you as much as I do." Only later did I learn, when I stumbled on a book called *Why Does He Do That? Inside the Minds of Angry and Controlling Men*, that this was classic abuser language. I was not unique, and I was not alone.

In the passenger seat of Julian's SUV one of the last times I saw him, I was about to get out at a corner on Union Square to go to a Halloween party (six years to the date of the one where I had proposed to Emir). I was dressed as Mrs. Bridge, the title character in Evan S. Connell's novel, the unsatisfied wife of a workaholic husband in the 1940s. I'd just finished the novel and loved it so much I created a costume of the main character, a perpetually disappointed woman with a constrained life. It was the perfect Halloween costume because it's a horror story—my own personal worst-case-scenario horror story. One my own middle age could have resembled if I didn't get out of the car. Sitting at that stoplight with Julian, I was simultaneously sad and relieved. For the first time since I was sixteen, the future was open. At twenty-seven, it finally became clear that there are no fairy tales or fated romances. I'd put all my stock in the concept of "soul mates," somehow convinced that Julian was mine. The concept made for a trap. Beautiful bars of gold up close—I held them, smooth and cool, in my hands. Only when I stepped away could I see the cage.

MARRIAGE IS AN act predicated on faith, because there is no telling if it will be what you think it is. I entered my first knowing it was "fake" and watched it turn real, while the second, entered with certainty of its realness, turned fake. Like a magic trick. And yet each had elements of both: Julian and I had sex, Emir and I did not. Emir and I loved each other no matter what. Julian's love came with gilded strings. Each man received a green card. One was supposed to be because of me, and one wasn't. Even this ended up strangely reversed.

After Julian's green card was finalized, unlike with the hugs and see-you-soons with Emir, the divorce process turned ugly: "I had a little meeting with the INS," Julian wrote, a veiled threat about Emir. Our lawyers yelled at each other across the table while Julian yelled at them both. When it was over, accounts separated and back taxes paid, we never spoke again. I didn't regret marrying Julian, though. I was finally free of an eleven-year-long obsession.

EMIR AND I walked around the East Village together again. He was there for me at a time when he stood to gain nothing. If it wasn't for our time married, we'd likely have gone our own ways and lost touch. Our union remained real even after it ended, a paradox revealing that there is no universal truth about marriage. We all need to customize our vows. Marriage is inherently transactional, but to what degree? Getting green cards, getting babies, getting a tax break, getting a house? Getting to bask in married glory in the aisles of Trader Joe's holding hands with your favorite person—or person to whom you are legally bound in that moment? Which kinds of love are real enough to warrant making "official," placing on a pedestal or in a hierarchy? I recently saw that a Facebook acquaintance bought a giant blue sapphire ring and "married" herself, including a link to a registry. Was that worth celebrating, too?

Emir's need for the green card motivated my proposal, but behind our "fake" marriage was love, in one of its many iterations. From him I learned about loving myself and loving another. I wanted a marriage like ours but with the romantic and sexual elements, a marriage of equals in which I wouldn't need a room of my own because my partner would be the kind of person who—no matter what his own profession—understood my needs (for time and solitude), took the kids to the playground, and shared the grocery shopping and household chores. And I would do the same for him.

I'd been married twice by age twenty-four, twice divorced by twenty-seven, and still knew not much about marriage. Except for one thing: if I did it again, Emir would walk me down the aisle for the third time. I wasn't anyone's to give away. But if I were, I'd choose him.

A note from the desk of

THE PROFILER

MY OWN DAUGHTER entering into a marriage of malfeasance to circumvent the U.S. immigration laws I so staunchly upheld in my diplomatic work. How could you do that, Liza?

When I found out that Liza had married Emir, I wasn't thinking about marriage rights or equality, "traditional" or "same-sex" unions. I was hurt, angry, and disappointed. I wasn't opposed to same-sex marriage, and several Foreign Service colleagues had same-sex partners. A few had even married in foreign countries that legally recognized such unions. But due to the Defense of Marriage Act (DOMA) we were prohibited from issuing an immigrant visa to a foreigner married to a U.S. citizen of the same gender, even if they had married legally in a consenting state or foreign nation. Signed into law in 1996 by President Bill Clinton, DOMA recognized marriage only between a man and a woman for federal purposes. Fortunately, this section of law was declared unconstitutional and overturned in 2013.

Eventually, my resentment subsided. Passing through New York between tours, I had brunch with Liza, Emir, and the guy he was dating. I liked Emir, who, by then, had become a U.S. citizen.

But Julian. Could profiling have helped her be more cautious? Intelligent, confident, and outgoing, with a sense of humor. Energetic and goal oriented, no doubt he would "go places" in his chosen financial career. But is a type-A dynamo easy to be around 24/7? While he met The Profiler's checklist of positives, and he and Liza seemed to be on the same wavelength, "expectations" is a key word.

Dating couples should share their views and hopes about how they imagine their married life together. People dismiss or brush aside an issue as "not really important," or think they can change the other person later. Liza thought Julian was fun, generous, and considerate. But were there signs of the domineering, impatient personality that would later emerge? With a more thoughtful, objective analysis, could Liza have noticed red flags early on?

The Profiler wants to throw out just a few more thoughts to consider. Respect and support are vital. Be sure to look for these traits in any potential partner. Encouraging each other to develop individually while growing bonds as a couple is not easy. Somewhere between high school in Mexico and careers in New York City, Julian and Liza's relationship changed. They became separated by conflicting expectations and individual goals. They clashed over issues both minor and major. Mutual support and respect disappeared. And love along with them. Watch out as you go along—be sure you are observing clues and signs along the way.

THE FAKE TRIP

THE CHANCE TO live abroad was the primary reason my mother chose her Foreign Service career. She wanted to experience the world, or at least the attractive parts of it. She instructed my teachers to give me class assignments to go so she could bring me along to London, Paris, the Dolomites for a ski trip, or a beach town that hadn't yet been ruined with tourists because of a feature in *The New York Times* Travel section. Trips offered an education in language, culture, open-mindedness—the real world.

"The great thing about growing up overseas is you can learn about history and art in class, and then go see what you read about in cities, ruins, and museums," she said.

A trip, she taught me, was the ultimate present. "A gift? Spend it on airplane tickets!" she'd say. "On experiences." Who needed things when adventures were the real treasure? It was one place we saw eye to eye. A promising romantic candidate would also understand the value of travel and surprise you with "a nice trip" for your birthday or just because. This was one of the reasons why The Profiler had approved my high-school-turned-Wall-Street ex-husband. He, too, traveled the globe constantly for work and pleasure and sometimes took me along.

NATHAN WAS HOSTING a reading series on one of my first nights of grad school. I noticed we had the same glasses, matching his-and-hers Versace frames. So often it's the little things, isn't it, that trigger a sensation of instant interest or connection? Something as meaningless as matching glasses reads as a sign. Nathan was so comfortable behind the podium. The whole crowd laughed at his jokes. It wasn't love or even lust at first sight—he was attractive in an offbeat way, with curly brown hair, a ruddy complexion, and chubby apple cheeks. But I wasn't thinking about that when a mutual acquaintance—Nathan's best friend, who had, coincidentally, dated one of my closest college girlfriends back in Boston (another one of those details to which I ascribed meaning—fate!)—introduced us.

One night, some classmates and I decided to go to the neighborhood bar where the grad students hung out. There, on a barstool, nursing a whiskey and a beer, sat Nathan. We spent the next few hours talking. Nathan was Midwestern. After Julian, his niceness alone made him a total catch. After he asked if we could see each other and I said yes, he took my new necklace with him, as if to secure the date.

A few days later, we went to a sidewalk café in Chelsea and ordered soup. We were coming down with something that was going around, or hungover, or some combination of both. When the check came, Nathan said, "Actually, ummm, I'm waiting on my student loans to come through. Can you cover this one?"

I experienced the twinge that The Profiler would have pointed out was my instinct telling me this was a red flag, but instead I put my credit card down.

"Can I at least have my necklace back, then?" I asked with a wink.

"I'm so sorry," he said. "It broke. I'll get you a new one."

"No! How?"

"In my jacket pocket. It somehow cracked in two."

"Promise you'll replace it when your loans come through?"

"Of course," he said.

As if to drive home that it didn't bother me, I offered to buy us a round of sangria at the Spanish bar around the corner. Nathan was not a trip-gifter. He was broke, sleeping on a friend's couch in Harlem. But I didn't want to be judgmental like The Profiler. I wouldn't write off a nice guy with potential at the first sign that he might not be perfect. Besides, he was ideal in other ways: Nathan came from an intact, sibling-filled family. He moved to New York City from the hometown where he'd lived all his life. Sure, he wasn't some sophisticated international traveler, but a lot more than that was needed for a relationship to work. Nathan knew a certain kind of stability I'd never had. He came from the type of family I idealized, the kind where everyone cried when they parted ways after holiday visits because they were going to miss each other.

When Nathan and I updated our relationship status a few weeks later, my phone rang immediately. Caller: MOM.

"I don't like that Nathan," she said, The Profiler in full effect.

"Stop Facebook stalking me."

"It doesn't look like he has a lot of money. Does he even have a job?"

"Stop. Profiling. Everyone."

"Looks like he drinks quite a bit."

"You're going off a few pictures that happen to be taken at a bar."

"Well, something's off."

"You've never even met him," I said.

"I don't need to. A profiler can tell."

"You mean a mother can."

I'd come up with other nicknames for her: Micro*mom*ager and S'mother. I refused to see a correlation between the kind of profiling she did for her work—a physical assessment followed by questioning—and her ability to make accurate snap judgments about the suitability of my suitors. She'd been wrong about Julian. Well, not entirely, since she'd recognized and pointed out his controlling, aggressive ways. But she'd put concerns aside because he was the youngest managing director on Wall Street. Sure, Nathan was far from the platonic form of responsibility, but every successful person started somewhere, and who was to say he wouldn't become an award-winning poet and tenured professor?

After years with a money-obsessed investment banker who liked to joke about when Citibank would "open their vaults" for the money I would someday make to prove my worth, Nathan's goals were refreshing. The red of his bank account was not a turnoff after all that pressure. Something The Profiler's tactics could not take into consideration was timing. I was happy to hole up at Nathan's, eating olives and cheese from the bodega while we worked in the darkness of a windowless room with a plastic table and chairs. For my birthday, he made good on his promise to get me another necklace like the one he'd accidentally broken.

After we'd been dating for a month, Nathan moved off his friend's couch and into a room in Prospect Heights, which in 2007 was still a Brooklyn neighborhood that was a draw because of its cheaper rent.

My mother would have been horrified, but she couldn't see the parts of my daily life that weren't posted on Facebook, and she couldn't deport Nathan back to Nebraska, where we were headed for Thanksgiving so I could meet his family.

Nathan's parents and siblings were warm and welcoming, and treated me as if I'd always been one of them. When Nathan first told me he was from Omaha, I pictured a red barn, fields, chickens, and cattle. He laughed and showed me Omaha's Wikipedia page, which featured a photograph of a real city. I apologized for my narrow-mindedness.

I took to Omaha as I did any foreign place. The zoo was amazing. There was a bar that served champagne on tap. The old downtown had great restaurants, chic boutiques, and an excellent bookstore with stocked shelves we perused for hours. Up late at his parents' house, binge-watching *Curb Your Enthusiasm*, Nathan and I snuggled under blankets. I felt content and at home. "You stay here," he said. "I'll go organize snacks." In the morning, his scientist mother taught me her favorite way to poach an egg, a simple technique I'd go on to use all the time.[3] To my own mother's ongoing horror, I could not wait to return to the place I'd affectionately nicknamed Homeaha.

BACK IN NEW York, over bottomless cups of coffee at the Hungarian café frequented by the graduate students, Nathan and I composed a running list in a small black Moleskine notebook of all the places we wanted to

---

3 Nebraskan Mother's Egg-Poaching Method: Heat a pot of water on the stove and watch until the small bubbles rise—not quite yet a simmer, definitely not a boil. That right there is the perfect moment and temperature to stir the water vigorously, creating a small whirlpool in the center. Crack the egg and drop it into the whirlpool. Watch as the water swirls around it, holding the egg at its center, unmoving. After a few minutes, scoop the egg out with a slotted spoon. Deposit the egg on buttered toast, sprinkle it with salt and fresh ground pepper, and enjoy. Thanks, Nathan's Mom!

travel: Portugal, Buenos Aires, Havana. He hadn't traveled internationally save a drunken college trip to Tijuana and wanted to go abroad. Then, we agreed, we'd move to some quaint college town after grad school, where we would find tenured professorships, write, and fill our days with books, pets, students, and elaborate vegetarian meals prepared from scratch.

My mother may not have become The Big Mom In The Sky, but she was The Little Mom In My Mind. The flaw in profiling, I lectured this imaginary mother lurking in my neurotransmitters, was that it didn't account for somebody's potential. Nathan hadn't been a traveler, but was enthused at the possibility, which was more important. He didn't do it because somebody raised him that way. He was in the process of becoming.

So there you have it, Little Mom In My Mind: Trips. Ivy League grad program. Stable Midwestern family. Wants to commit. And can I say it again? Trips. Once he gets out of debt he'll probably even give me one for my birthday. In the meantime, I'll take care of us.

And that's how, two months later, over our December break, Nathan and I tackled two of the places on our to-trip list: the Mayan Riviera (already one of my favorite places) and Havana, accessed on my Italian passport and stampless on his newly procured American one, via Cancun. "I bet that guy doesn't even have a passport," The Profiler said disapprovingly before we left on this voyage that troubled her immensely, though I'd told her only of our Mexico plan, not Cuba. "Of course he does, Mom," I retorted, belligerent. It wasn't a lie, exactly. We were standing in the post office right then taking care of the paperwork. "And he's been to Mexico before," I added.

It didn't matter. I already had a fantasy of Nathan and me becoming a present-day version of Joan Didion—my literary idol—and John Gregory Dunne, that magical, matched pair of revered writers who took a lot of trips.

Nathan was easy to travel with, a natural at the brand of planned spontaneity The Profiler had instilled as our travel style. We wandered all over Havana on foot, eating street pizza and sampling mojitos from every charming little bar. A guard at the Hemingway house tried to sell us "one of Hemingway's paper clips" for a cool hundred dollars. We doubled over in laughter as we made our way back to the crammed bus that would return us to our *casa particular* for an afternoon siesta. We got confused and conned over the two kinds of legal tender, the peso and convertible peso, and laughed a little less about what we realized were our fifty-dollar bowls of ice cream. The return flight to Cancun was on a plane so old and rickety that I experienced what the airport doctor in Cancun referred to as a "traumatic eardrum event." After peering into my ear, he forbade me to fly for a week lest the eardrum rupture. We checked into the Hyatt, finding that my bad luck was a blessing: We got to spend an extra week on vacation in Cancun, where, to my surprise and dismay, I discovered that Señor Frog's and Applebee's were a welcome relief after time on the communist island, where even sandwiches had been scarce. We returned to freezing Brooklyn on Christmas Day and ordered in Chinese. Nathan acted withdrawn all day, and I started to worry, but when I finally asked why later that evening, he admitted he was sad about his first Christmas spent away from his family.

We took more trips, to South Africa and New Orleans. I figured one day he would return the favor, but until then I was fine—happy, even—with covering our adventures to places on our list. The only thing that bothered me was that Nathan always found money for cigarettes. But that was a physical addiction, I rationalized, not reading the obvious smoke signal that would have sent rescuers flocking to that island. He would quit, I knew.

The Profiler swept in to visit from Caracas, Venezuela, where she was stationed at the height of Chavez's reign. She stayed at my great-uncle's in Chelsea and asked Nathan and me to meet for lunch at a nearby French bistro. She wore a monochromatic pantsuit, and her hair, naturally dark like mine, was blown out and lightened, more like Hillary Clinton's than usual.

NATHAN AND THE Profiler exchanged pleasantries as we waited for our table. We sat, we ordered french onion soup, and Nathan excused himself to go to the restroom. Did The Profiler make him nervous? He was on edge. Her judging gaze was intimidating. I feared he was exhibiting the very traits that would stir her criticism—lack of confidence and self-assuredness, avoidance, etc. My ex-husband was her energetic and intellectual equal. She could spar with him about stocks and travel and world affairs. Nathan The Gentle Poet had no chance of living up to that in her mind, but where did kindness vs. aggression rank on her who's-right-for-you scale? She hadn't seen the Meanball in Julian. Or perhaps it was more that she, like me, didn't really want to see it because the rest of him was so ideal. She pierced the solid cheese surface of her soup with a steak knife.

"I was right," she said. "Something's off."

I glanced to the back of the restaurant to where Nathan had disappeared behind a heavy wooden door. I jabbed at the surface of my own soup with my own knife.

"You just met him," I said, watching the brown liquid, soggy bread, and steam rise to the surface of the bowl.

"That's all the time I need to tell you that something about him is not right."

"Stop micromomaging already. Why can't we just have a nice lunch?"

"Because you make bad decisions and I hate seeing you waste your time. He's slovenly, schleppy, disheveled—"

"Mom, that's all the same thing."

"—arrogant, and a moocher who will take advantage of you. He thinks he's a poet."

"He *is* a poet. He got into an Ivy League university for his poetry."

"Maybe he pulled the wool over their eyes, too."

I didn't want The Profiler to be right. I wanted to be in love, and love wasn't logical. She was trying to speak to love with the logic of the mind. There was no set of qualities an "applicant" could meet to be the right life partner. Choosing a partner was not a simple or straightforward yes-or-no process like a visa interview. Even back then I told her as much.

When Nathan rejoined us at the table, The Profiler was pleasant enough, but I knew when she was faking. I steamed more and longer than that bowl of soup. How could she be so judgmental? The problem wasn't Nathan and it wasn't me, I thought back at that ill-fated lunch. It was *her*.

After the meal, I'd conceded to a hair appointment, on my mother's request, in which the stylist would strip the black dye I'd had done over the summer. This process would take many hours. From the chair I watched my mother and Nathan sitting over on the bench in the waiting area. They weren't speaking. She was looking at a magazine while he sat immersed in a text on poetics. The chemicals burned my nose and scalp. Why had I agreed to this? Just so my mother would stop nagging me about my hair? When I emerged, hours later, the sky was black and my hair was back to brown. Nathan ducked out to buy a pack of cigarettes, quietly as I'd warned him not to be open about smoking with The Profiler.

"Are you happy now?" I asked.

"I can't believe he sat here the whole time you were getting your hair done," she said.

"He *likes* being around me, Mom."

"He's an entitled hanger-on with an attitude."

I DID NEXT what any good rebellious daughter would do: ignored my mother's advice and asked Nathan to move in. Since Nathan was still waiting on his next round of student loans, I would handle rent while Julian awaited his green card, and we could split it afterward.

NATHAN AND I commenced the apartment search in Brooklyn. Nothing was quite right. The apartments were in rough neighborhoods, or too small, or too expensive. Then I saw it. Every New York apartment search goes something like this: the moment you're about to give up, it reveals itself. The right one. It was in Prospect Heights, on the same street where Nathan had moved, but a block closer to the subway and Flatbush Avenue. It was a light-filled, full second floor of a brownstone.

Something had to be wrong with it for it to be, at $1,600 a month, so affordable. The Profiler would certainly say so. Or so said The Little Mom In My Mind.

We went to look at it one evening after class, emerging from the subway at the 7th Avenue stop in Park Slope. The air smelled of fried chicken from a Spanish restaurant, and the streets were filled with the sound of drumming and call-and-response singing from what I assumed was an African dance class in a studio above the subway station. Half a block down Carlton Avenue and there was the brownstone, second from the corner, a little more run down than the others but still beautiful.

Upstairs, there was a living room with a separate kitchen, a hallway with two closets that were huge by New York standards closets, an office with a bathroom, and a separate sleeping nook too small to be called a room, though by New York standards, it was a room. The one deceptive thing about the apartment was the flooring, which was linoleum designed to look like hardwood. This was worse than straightup linoleum that didn't try to disguise itself. There was fakery between these walls.

For this place, though, I'd be willing to live with it.

We filled out forms for the broker. Nettie and Bernie, the ancient landlords who lived in the apartment downstairs, arrived. The larger problem surfaced along with them.

"Are these two married?" Bernie asked the broker. "We're Jehovah's Witnesses. We want a married couple in here."

The broker sighed. Bernie's request was illegal. The broker was about to argue when I chimed in with a swifter solution—and one more likely to get us the apartment.

"We're engaged," I said. "We're actually getting married next week."

Nathan didn't miss a beat. "On some land I own back in Nebraska," he chimed in.

"The ring is just out getting resized," I explained.

Nettie and Bernie exchanged an approving glance and invited us back for a proper interview.

"You nailed it in there," I said to Nathan as we walked back to the train.

He high-fived me. "Nice job, counterpart!"

"Yeah, 'some land I own back in Nebraska'? Good one. What they were doing is totally illegal anyway, so it doesn't matter that we lied."

"It's not lying," he said. "It's just creating a new reality for another person," he said.

I RETURNED TWO days later wearing my old engagement ring. They handed me the lease.

"You're making a big mistake," The Profiler said.

When we moved into the perfect apartment (if you ignored the fake linoleum, plumbing issues, and roaches crawling out of the crack in the kitchen wall), Nathan brought over two army rucksacks containing clothes, an old laptop, books, and a waffle iron. Since my mother was a single mom who had supported a child on her own, she wanted me to find a man who would support me, who would give me the wifely life she didn't have. But there were no longer gendered conventions for couples' financial arrangements, and it was empowering to be the one who could support my boyfriend (for now). When Nathan became a professor who published poetry in *The New Yorker* after graduate school, he would have a turn. It was perfect fairness: we'd trade off between who was teaching and who was writing full-time. We were practicing for that now. In line with my fantasy that we could be some next-gen version of my idols of literary coupledom, I procured matching desks and chairs. We set them up in the office to face each other as we wrote, something that nauseated our grad school friends when they came to the parties we regularly threw. We even began collaborating on a detective story screenplay, more like J.D. and J.G.D. than ever. We played backgammon, cooked "colorful veggie chili," and prepared what we termed The Giant Salad: mixed lettuce, tomatoes, corn, beets, hearts of palm, cheese, olives, and the occasional avocado, smothered in Goddess dressing. These were our Giant Salad Days. We would finish our screenplay, sell it to Hollywood, write our books, and find success as a literary power couple. I was divorcing. He was in debt. What direction was there for us to go but up?

My mother had the mistaken idea of Nathan as a "sports-watching couch potato" because once when she visited the apartment, on a Sunday afternoon, Nebraska was playing football. Nathan was watching with a bottle of beer. She assumed things were always as they were the few times she was around. Unfortunately, she only seemed to visit when Nebraska football was on TV, as if she were psychic and timed her visits to encounter this "proof" of Nathan's unworthiness. I tried to explain to her that he was not a "couch potato" and didn't spend all his time watching sports and drinking beer. He was an intellectual. He loved me. He would be a professor soon. And would quit smoking, too.

For a while, his smoking was our only argument. Then I got a filing cabinet. While organizing papers I came across a letter from the attorneys of the university trustees. Nathan was being sued for $8,032.08 in unpaid rent for student housing the year before I met him. This was how he ended up on his friend's couch. He'd never told me. When I confronted him, he admitted his parents had paid off the debt.

"How could you do that?" I asked.

"How can you nag me about something that happened and got resolved before we even met?"

He was working on changing his habits. Why couldn't I back off and let him?

As The Profiler's daughter, I'd made it my mission not to advise anybody else on what to do, so I let it go.

THE SUMMER AFTER my first year of grad school, my novel, a fictionalized story that took place in the *Gossip Girl*–meets–Mexico City high school I attended, was released. My dream-turned-reality, though, was soon accompanied by tragedy. In July, the month after its publication, my estranged father died of alcoholic liver failure in Italy. I couldn't get there in time for the funeral, so I didn't go at all. It felt unreal. My father hadn't responded to my letters in years. I also grieved the loss of potential reconciliation that died along with him. Nathan became my source of comfort. He held me as I cried on the Pottery Barn carpet I'd bought to cover the fake-linoleum floor. It had always felt as if my mother was my one parent. Now she really was. She always said she never regretted marrying him because she had me. I wondered how much her experience of marriage contributed to her overinvolvement in my relationships.

I went to Miami the week after my father's death to give a reading. My mother flew up from Caracas. We signed and FedExed some forms to my father's brother in Italy to absolve me of responsibility for my father's debt. This was a relief since I was already invested in another man with debt.

When I got home, he and I picked up a black pug puppy from the Continental Airlines freight cargo building after a confused and panicked hour at baggage claim. I named her Baxter, which in Middle English means "female baker," and she resembled a little bread loaf. I wouldn't remember until later that Nathan and I had also just watched the Michael Showalter movie *The Baxter*—the title of which, ironically, refers to the guy in a romantic comedy whom you *don't* want the heroine to end up with. The pug, with her silly face and tongue that hung out only one side of her head, provided the closest thing to comfort in the surreal grief I felt for a father who was reduced to a childhood memory of a smiling Italian man whose foot I latched on to every evening as he tried to leave for his restaurant job.

MY LAST SEMESTER of grad school, I took a widely loved class about the nature of memory and imagination in nonfiction, nicknamed Truth Class. James Frey, the notorious memoirist who lied to Oprah, was a guest speaker. He became famous for his first book and more famous when it came out he'd invented some things. My generation's literary scandal. His talk at Truth Class was unlike anything else I'd heard in grad school, peppered with advice along the lines of, "When you stop giving a fuck is when you'll write something great." We listened to his take on the scandal: He had been vilified—and by Oprah, which basically made him the devil—chased through his neighborhood by paparazzi, followed to his kid's school. It got so intense that the Frey family ended up expatriating for a while. He'd put it all behind him and had a new novel coming out. We all have our own truths, our own versions of "the story," and that was his. The valuable takeaway, for me at least, was that no matter how deep a humiliation we experience, human beings have an incredible ability to bounce back.

I WAS TURNING thirty in November. Nathan and I had been together for nearly three years. We would both have our shiny new grad school degrees soon. My divorce finally came through. Nathan got a part-time job as a secretary at an architecture office. He would chip away at his debt and help with our household expenses. For my thirtieth birthday, he revealed he'd gotten me a trip to the Florida Keys in February, for a long weekend that culminated with Valentine's Day. I was so proud. A trip! What could The Profiler say now?

Gray snow lined the streets of Brooklyn. I tried to extract details about Nathan's secret birthday trip.

"Are we staying in a boutique hotel, or somewhere more like the Hyatt?" I quizzed him.

"More like the Hyatt," he said.

"Is the flight in the morning or afternoon?"

"Afternoon."

"Oh good."

"What books are you going to bring for the beach?" he asked.

I dashed over to our bookshelf to have a look. Nathan had been encouraging me to read some of the experimental poetry on his side of the shelf. I reached for one of those.

As the weekend of the trip approached, I breathed for Key West. I sat squished between a fat man and a fat man on the subway for an hour on my way uptown, where I was teaching a freshman composition class. I told my students I'd be unavailable for Thursday's office hours because of the birthday-slash-Valentine's trip my boyfriend had planned. My gift to Nathan would be nice dinners out in Key West. One of my students gave me a restaurant recommendation. We talked about the six-toed cats at the Hemingway house, the second Hemingway house Nathan and I would visit together, as if the hand of fate was nudging us toward our literary destiny.

After class, I met Emir outside the Marc Jacobs store in the West Village. His partner was one of the architects for the store. With his discount, I purchased a pricey but beautiful swimsuit for Key West, a modest but sexy one-piece. As I modeled it for Nathan back at the apartment, he agreed it was the absolute perfect thing for our trip.

I went to the sleeping nook to pack.

That evening, as I shuffled around getting last-minute things ready—toothbrushes, a few more books—I noticed Nathan was spending a lot of time on his computer. Inspired writing session, I figured, as the deadline for his thesis was rapidly approaching and he'd taken to redoing his poems. Later, when I glanced at the screen over his shoulder while pausing to give him a kiss, he tried to close a browser window fast. But I'd already seen it: Priceline. A search for airline tickets to Trinidad/Tobago. And Ecuador. And the Dominican Republic.

"What are you doing?" I asked, my voice quivering because as much as I hoped there was some other explanation, some future romantic trip he was already starting to plan, I already knew.

Nathan said nothing.

Then he said he'd accidentally screwed up the dates for Key West, the tickets were actually for the following month, and he didn't want to disappoint me so he was looking for a trip we could take tomorrow.

"There never was a trip, was there," I said.

"No," he admitted.

"You got me a fake trip for my thirtieth birthday."

"I really meant to make it happen."

"The night before?"

"I couldn't afford it and thought there might be some last-minute sales."

"You know who can afford last-minute travel? Rich people! They can buy plane tickets the night before. Or at least people whose credit cards aren't all cancelled!"

"I'm sorry. I'm not your investment banker ex."

"You lied for months!"

How far had he been going to take it? How long had he planned to wait, especially after this last-ditch effort fell through? Until the morning we were supposed to leave? Would he have made up some crazy story on the ride to the airport? When would he have told me, if I hadn't walked in? The Fake Trip was humiliating, as was Nathan's trying to take his lie and make it true somehow. When, while we were deceiving our Jehovah's Witness landlords, Nathan had said lying is "just creating a new reality for another person," I'd thought he was joking. The biggest lie had been the one I'd told myself, that Nathan would become a person he was not. Coming from a stable family didn't guarantee someone was stable. The Profiler would have told me that.

No, we were not becoming what I'd hoped, not at all.

I took out my emergency Amex, for this counted as an emergency. I would go eat the key lime pie at that restaurant, go pet the six-toed cats at the Hemingway house. Go on the trip I'd thought I was taking, but alone. "A trip alone is better than one with the wrong person," I imagined my mother would say if I told her.

I did tell Nathan I wanted him gone by the time I got back.

NATHAN WAS NOT gone when I got back. I asked again why he'd decided to lie for months when the truth, while not what either of us wanted, would have been easier.

"I had every intention of righting the situation," he said.

"How?"

"My loans would come through . . . I'd be able to save more . . . I don't know."

I should have known that Nathan couldn't afford a trip. We were both liars. He lied to me, and I lied to myself. Sunburned skin comes off, underneath, more skin.

A cardinal rule of personal essay and memoir is that the narrator must critique, judge, and investigate the self more than anyone else in the piece. Or as one writer I admire put it, "You have to be the biggest asshole in your story." Nathan made that hard. But I was the one who had chosen to be with him. Who had chosen to ignore the signs. So maybe I'm the real asshole after all.

Nathan showed up drunk in a penguin suit for one of our early dates (granted, it was to a costume party), spilling flowers on the floor of my sublet room. Instead of throwing him out, I made him promise not to show up drunk again. (When he was subsequently drunk, I worried and fretted and forgave.) He slept over and had brought nothing to wear the next day but this penguin suit with no pants. (*Lack of foresight and planning*, said The Little Mom In My Mind. *Undesirable traits in a partner*.) Rather than sending him off to ride the subway in the long polyester dress of his penguin suit, I took him to an expensive *man*tique on the Lower East Side and bought him two-hundred-dollar Lower East Side mantique jeans, rationalizing that he looked good in them and would have them forever. Back then I somehow thought he'd have me forever, too, which would have made the jeans a good investment. I was still trying to save somebody, or fix him. The Profiler was right. But what I thought, because I would listen to anyone before I'd admit my mother had been right, was that when it mattered, James Frey spoke the truth.

A PROFESSOR, TWO grad students, and James Frey walk into an Indian restaurant. It sounds like the setup of a bad joke, but this happened a few evenings after I returned from The Real Fake Trip. I recounted The Fake Trip to James Frey, trying to take it from minor tragedy to funny story.

"He is *not* marriage material," James Frey said.

James Frey knew an unforgivable lie when he heard one. I realized that the boyfriend to whom I'd devoted the last three years of my life was less trustworthy than the man famous for LYING TO OPRAH.

Though I'd told Nathan to move out, being me, I was wavering, verging on making excuses for him again even though I knew I could not spend my life with the man who gave me The Fake Trip.

I'd rather James Frey pointed it out than The Profiler. I still couldn't get up the nerve to tell her about The Fake Trip. Not only would she be devastated—a trip, of all things!—but also she would say, "I was right . . . I warned you about that Nathan and now look, you wasted years and money on a guy who gave you a fake trip . . ."

"WHEN ARE YOU moving out?" I asked Nathan.

"I'm not," he said. "You move out."

"Excuse me?"

"I like living here," he said. "If you want to leave, then go."

"But how will you afford this place on your own . . . ?"

I paused. When had that ever stopped him? He would squat until the old Jehovah's Witnesses could figure out how to evict him, a process that would surely take forever. He did it with the campus housing. He could do it again.

Why hadn't I understood sooner what my mother clearly saw about Nathan? Heeding her counsel would have saved me a lot of time, money, and trouble. But as Hemingway said, "The best way to find out if you can trust somebody is to trust them." Can there be another way to know if you're meant to be with someone than to be with them? A relationship that doesn't work out—or works out disastrously—isn't necessarily a waste. There is a lesson in it at least, even if that lesson is, don't keep dating the guy who shows up drunk in a penguin suit.

Even if the lesson is, listen to your mother.

At thirty, though, I didn't want her input on my every decision. She could find a reason why anyone wasn't right. Typically, I would have glossed over the reason for a breakup out of fear of her judgment or criticism. "Why couldn't you see it coming? I told you . . ." A lecture on my poor decision making. But I'd made a resolution in light of The Fake Trip. Having been lied to for months by the person I loved, I promised myself I would not "create a new reality" for my mother (or future landlords, or anyone) again. I vowed to myself to try to be as honest and forthcoming as possible about all things. Truth was far less exhausting than the efforts required to maintain a fiction—Nathan had taught me that much.

When I told my mother, she wasn't irritated, or at least not, as I had suspected she would be, with me.

"He gave you a what?" she said. "What a liar! Well you're not the first one to fall for a deceitful guy."

Then my mother did something that is rare for her. She told me a story.

"Remember Alberto? You met him in Rome?"

"Vaguely, yeah."

"He was the biggest crush of my life. I met him my sophomore year at Stanford, in the autumn of 1969. He showed up at the Stanford villa where we stayed outside of Florence. I *really* liked him. We'd go out dancing and to dinner, I'd skip a history of Italian politics class to go stand near the one phone for the students to use and wait for his calls. We were having a great time. Little did I know—he was married! He had a wife and a kid. This other guy, Stefano, who liked me, brought me a copy of Alberto's family status document he got from City Hall."

The Profiler's first document of deception—years before she became The Profiler! I'd never heard much from her archive of love gone wrong.

"Awful. Did you confront him? What did he have to say for himself?"

"I don't remember. It was over forty years ago. But I was mostly really sad. We saw each other in Italy over the course of the years—he was divorced then but always had lots of women. You just don't have perspective when you're in something. It only comes later on, when you can see the situation as an outsider."

My mother also learned from experience that someone she was in love with had been lying for months. I imagined Stefano bringing my mother the copy of Alberto's Italian family status certificate, revealing that her great love was a cheating married man with a family. The young woman who was not yet my mother poring over it in the courtyard of the Florentine villa, seeking any sign that it could have been forged.

"After Stefano brought you the marriage document, did you go out with him?" I asked.

"I did. He was in the wine industry, and we traveled around Tuscany. He was nice. But I didn't feel passionate about him like I did about Alberto."

We'd both been deceived, but really we had deceived ourselves because we had wanted to be in love, and love isn't logical. Perhaps we all ignore our profiling "powers" in the face of great passion. In retrospect, I should have listened to my mother and at least not let Nathan move in, but I'd also taken some of her advice. I'd spent my money on an experience. And gotten a trip out of it.

A note from the desk of

THE PROFILER

THE MOMENT I laid my eyes on Nathan, I knew he wasn't the one. He was *one* to immediately run away from! What my daughter saw in him—who knows. What The Profiler saw was a disheveled, unkempt guy (check overall appearance). Wimpy handshake and averted eyes (insecure/lack of self-confidence). No charisma or character. Only a bit of arrogance. It got worse from there. His conversational interjections were few, and he had an unpleasant habit of twirling a finger in his curly hair. And no energy. The Profiler saw it all—in an instant.

Liza, what didn't you see? All the nonverbal and other signs were quite obvious. Not a Mr. Right! A Mr. Big Mistake. And then, I didn't even know she was footing all the bills. That makes me angry even now!

Don't waste precious time: run from bad choices.

Stop a moment and Think (with a capital *T*). What kind of partner—or first date—do you want? Though their looks might set your heart atwitter, don't just react to appearance. Observe. Look at verbal and nonverbal cues: how they interact with others, how they speak, overall demeanor. Kind, respectful, smart and honest? Shy or extroverted? A leader or a follower? What type is a better match for you? Profiling techniques are there for you. If you're looking for that special someone, take a look at the first appendix and start practicing. You'll learn a lot about people—and be surprised how easy it is, and how useful for daily life.

SEEING AS YOUR SHOES ARE SOON TO BE ON FIRE

AMONG THE THINGS I pull from the bathtub are fourteen years of journals. Along with the contents of the filing cabinet—all the documents and records that make up a life—the pages of these journals are soaked in a mixture of water, triple sec, and what might be but I hope isn't urine. The ink on the pages is streaked into a blur of black and blue. The cops tell me I'm lucky that I am not. He would never be physically violent, I tell them. This is physical violence, they say.

Were this one of my mother's cases, she would have agreed.

One of the remaining legible lines inside the cover of the diary I kept the year I was twenty reads: "Zen thought du jour: All of our possessions are but Dumbo's feathers. You don't really need them."

This scrawling of my college self proves more prescient than I could have known—an oracle, a prophecy, or at least wise advice from someone who had no way of knowing that, ten years later, she would return home to her Brooklyn apartment on a Monday night to find that her recent ex had destroyed almost all her possessions. A whole ragged pile of Dumbo's feathers waiting in her apartment.

REWIND A WEEK or two: Nathan stalls, waiting to see if I'll let The Fake Trip blow over. I assure him it will not.

Then Nathan's refusal to leave. With classes to teach and a thesis due, I plan to go ostrich for the next three weeks, bury my head in the sand of work until the semester ends and I can properly focus on getting

Nathan to move out. His apologetic demeanor about the whole thing makes it somewhat tolerable, anyway, and then he leaves to spend a few days back in Nebraska for a family thing. I already know I'll miss his sweet family and those Omaha visits more than the man who'd brought me there to begin with.

Everything feels lighter after Nathan leaves. I make coffee alone and walk Baxter around the neighborhood on the warming spring mornings wishing Nathan would pack his rucksack of clothes, books, and waffle iron and go for good. The floor-through brownstone apartment, while still decrepit, would be all mine.

I MET THE Helicopter Pilot, a friend of a friend, three years earlier during a summer spent in Florida, when he was just about to move north to start his job flying tours over Manhattan. He offered me a spot on the tour sometime, but I took it for one of those things people say and don't follow through on. Until this.

I'm out walking the dog when my phone beeps in a text. The Helicopter Pilot: "Spot opened up on the afternoon tour, want to go for a ride?" When he meets me on the landing pad, I notice how handsome The Helicopter Pilot is: dark eyed, half-Portuguese, and extremely fit from his previous career as a professional *capoeirista*. Capoeira, he explains to me, is an Afro-Brazilian dance–acrobatic martial art, and I realize that's what goes on in the studio half a block from my apartment, though I never paid it any mind. The Helicopter Pilot had toured in Vegas and all over the country with his group and still practices recreationally. He is impressive: here is a man who is in control as he expertly lifts us off into the sky, the two of us in front, some German tourists in the backseat. He's entrusted with people's lives.

The Profiler, right again: why did I waste time trying to fix Nathan when there are men like The Helicopter Pilot in the world?

When we touch back down, he asks if I want to get together when he finishes work, and we reunite at a Cuban restaurant in my neighborhood, where we talk about travel, politics, books. The next day on campus, I sit on the grass watching tour helicopters circle in the sky and smile at knowing he is up there. Something in me is waking up after a long hibernation. It's springtime inside and out. We meet again a few days later and take a walk on a sunny afternoon. We trade funny stories about terrible exes and kiss when he leaves me at the subway stop to drive back to Jersey, where he lives. I know this is something, the elated, early rush of new romance, a blank slate, a fresh start.

I casually mention The Helicopter Pilot to The Profiler during our Sunday phone call.

"You were right," I tell her. "I'm starting to see this great new guy, a helicopter pilot—"

"Nope, not right for you," she says.

"Excuse me? You don't even know his name!"

"You won't have enough in common. That helicopter pilot isn't for you."

"That's so reductive. He's got a slew of intellectual interests. You haven't even done your Facebook stalking."

Because she was right about Nathan, her confidence is at an all-time high. I want her support—I want her to believe I can make good decisions—but how can she REJECT The Helicopter Pilot without even a glance at his Google hits?

BY THE TIME Nathan returns, I'm meeting The Helicopter Pilot for our fifth date at Franklin Park, a bar in Crown Heights with a huge outdoor patio. I tell Nathan. Impetus to move out.

"That guy?" he says when I explain who it is. They'd met once at a bar when the mutual friend who introduced me to The Helicopter Pilot came to town. "That guy is a douche bag."

"You're mad that I'm dating someone."

Nathan calls at five as I'm heading out to meet The Helicopter Pilot. With bar noise cluttering the background of the call, I can hear only well enough to know he's already drunk. He's yelling incoherently. I hang up. *No more men with drinking problems.*

Another point for The Helicopter Pilot: he drinks one glass of sauvignon blanc when we go out. Further evidence of responsibility and self-control. I'm not my mother, but am confident I'm profiling correctly this time. I put on lipstick and grab my purse.

Just before I walk out the door, an email pops up on my laptop from one of my students, saying a recommender for her application to the Telluride Film Festival Student Symposium has fallen through at the last minute. Do I have time to write a recommendation by midnight? I might not be back, but if I am, I certainly will! I place my computer on the dining table as a reminder to write the recommendation as soon as I walk in the door post–Helicopter Pilot date. A strange and sudden thought passes through my mind: *Don't leave that there. Hide it.* What? *What does that even mean?* my consciousness responds. I leave the computer on the table and go.

ON THE BUSTLING outdoor patio, The Helicopter Pilot sits at a picnic table, a glass of white wine in front of him and another awaiting my arrival. So thoughtful! And finally—a guy who likes wine, not another bad whiskey drunk. We sit side by side on the bench, our fingers intertwined, for hours. We have such an easy rapport.

It's half an hour to midnight as we settle our tab. I can still get home in time to fire off a recommendation for my student. I take my phone out to send her a message when I see a string of missed calls and voicemails from Nathan and a few from my closest friends.

Of the several messages left, it is this one from Nathan that strikes me the hardest: "Sorry you can't come to the phone right now, seeing as your shoes are soon to be on fire . . . I hate you, hope you die. Yeah, you'll probably die. So there's that for you."

"Nathan left me some strange voicemails, and he's been calling my friends," I tell The Helicopter Pilot, my hands trembling. I play the messages for him.

"Seeing as your shoes are soon to be on fire? What does that even mean?" he says. "Come on, let's go, I'll check it out with you."

I have him wait in the car while I go upstairs to investigate, The Helicopter Pilot at the ready for my call to come up if I need him. The couch is blocking the door, I realize as I push my way in. Nathan's sitting there, absent-mindedly smoking a cigarette in the living room, his eyes glassy and out of it, yet appearing content, even smug. Calm. This calmness which I'd initially admired as an ideal quality is the creepiest thing, more frightening than rage. I know right away he isn't going to come after me. His violence has been contained to inanimate objects. The dog cowers in the corner, afraid but—thank god—unharmed. I pick her up, relieved, though the biggest shock is still ahead. All the lights are on, and heavy metal music blares from the television. Nathan remains stoic as I walk around the apartment, shaking at the sight of what he's done. My clothes are strewn everywhere, reduced to shreds. Dresses look as if they've been attacked by a pack of wolverines. Shards of glass, torn-up papers, and destroyed artwork are drenched on the floors. My acoustic guitar is smashed to pieces.

The worst of it is in the bathroom. The bathtub is filled with water and years' worth of my journals and the contents of my filing cabinet. Underneath are family photographs—some of the only ones I have of my father. My parents' wedding invitation. And then, my laptop, and the smaller laptop I used for traveling. All drenched, all ruined. My student isn't getting her recommendation email tonight. Good thing I told her to find a backup. I should have, too—backed up, that is. My files. My whole thesis is gone.

I picture the MasterCard commercial. Computer: $1,500. Gucci dress for special events: $800. Guitar: $500. Voicemail from drunk crazy ex, "Sorry you can't come to the phone right now, seeing as your shoes are soon to be on fire": priceless.

What shoes did he burn? I run around with the dog in one arm, trying to collect anything salvageable in the other. Nathan still sits, smug, saying nothing. Where are the landlords?

("We're black, and we've lived here since the seventies, we don't call the cops," their daughter will later tell me. "If there's trouble you stay in and mind your business.")

"This property is your business!" I'll say, but she'll shake her head, and I will grasp the limitations of my understanding.)

I RUN BACK outside to The Helicopter Pilot and tell him about The Destruction, about Nathan sitting there in a daze.

"What are you waiting for? Call the cops," he says.

In my state of shock, the logical thing to do has escaped me. I dial 911. Three cops and an ambulance show up within minutes. Nathan is taken. Not arrested, but escorted into the ambulance. During our final months together, he started taking a combination of prescription drugs, Adderall and Zoloft, thanks to a psychiatrist who must not have had any idea about his whiskey intake. It turns out that, because I've given the police this information when they ask about "the suspect's" mental history, they'll take him to the hospital for psychiatric evaluation rather than slapping on handcuffs. I glimpse him through the ambulance glass. He's making the EMT laugh. Already charming his way out. He always could get everyone laughing with his quick wit. Everyone except The Profiler.

CLEARING THROUGH THE wreckage as the cops photograph the damage, I discover a little altar atop the backgammon board, a tarot card at its center: the knight of swords, a scrap of paper reading "Heroic Action." Nathan and I had pulled tarot cards one night from a deck I'd been inspired to buy after an appointment with the by-referral-only tarot card reader I visit annually. We were asking the cards about our future. I'd drawn the ten of cups and flipped through the interpretive guide: "A Good Marriage." He'd pulled the knight of swords: "Heroic Action." A shiver runs through me, and I wonder whether you can ever anticipate something like this, that someone you loved and who loved you—even if love is like pain in that you can no longer imagine or remember what it felt like when it's gone—is capable of such a display of hatred. It's so easy to see foreshadowing, warning signs, and commonsense indicators of trouble in the aftermath. Other cards left on Nathan's screwed-up little altar: the three of swords ("Flight of a Lady's Lover") and seven of swords ("Scandal for a Woman"). He'd taken the time to find these cards in the deck.

I LOCATE THE subject of that "seeing as your shoes are soon to be on fire" message. They're not even shoes. At least not just any shoes. He's attempted to char my beloved Accomplishment Boots.

I purchased the boots to celebrate selling my novel. I'd seen the boots everywhere that fall, in every magazine and fashion spread—shiny black leather, six-inch platform wedges. What sold me on them was the bottom latch looped through an opening in the wedge heel, a design detail I hadn't seen in all of my years as a shoe hound. They cost a thousand dollars. This was absolutely ludicrous. I could never otherwise justify paying a thousand dollars for a pair of boots, but it was a celebration of a goal I'd thought I might have a shot at reaching in my forties at the earliest. Besides, I justified, I'd have the boots forever. I would never need another pair. An investment. I reach into the boots, pull out wads of charred tissue.

Sergeant Tinajero finishes his photographs and informs me the damage is substantial. It is imperative that I follow this up in Family Court and get an order of protection, a restraining order. There is talk of mental histories and medications and psychotic breaks. Because Nathan is under the care of a psychiatrist and went to the hospital, he can no longer be arrested.

"But he committed a crime, didn't he? Don't people who commit crimes get arrested?"

Tinajero hands me a couple sheets of domestic incident report on pink carbon paper to sign. "Party #2 removed to Methodist via bus #31 Henry because of prior mental history."

"At least can I add these boots to the inventory of damaged property?"

THE HELICOPTER PILOT helps pick through the remains. It's a strange feeling, to be growing closer to him as we deal with cops, the flooded apartment, and boots charred on the inside.

"You should put in that report about how he endangered her dog," The Helicopter Pilot says to Tinajero, who scribbles it in.

I discover that Nathan has also stolen two thousand euros from my secret hiding place, a box wedged into the bottom of the bookshelf. If this is karmic retribution for the time I stole money from my mother's secret desk drawer to pay off a cop in Mexico City, it's almost too perfect. I had the euros from our trip to South Africa. They were a reimbursement from an airline for an overbooked flight. Why didn't I deposit the euros in the bank? Why didn't I listen to the little voice and move the computer? In retrospect, every step leading to here was a preventable accident.

"Can I stay at your place tonight?" I ask The Helicopter Pilot. It's nearly four in the morning. We're exhausted. The apartment is still in no condition. The lock on the front door is broken.

He hesitates.

"I just need a place to sleep," I say. I wonder if he misunderstands my intentions. Though on a night like this, what else could he think I want?

He relents and agrees. I figure he's just as shocked as I am. Destructive, psychotic ex-boyfriends aren't exactly what you expect to encounter on a fifth date. The Helicopter Pilot drives us over the Washington Bridge into New Jersey, to his apartment just on the other side of the river. His place is nice. Clean. He has a beautiful, well-behaved dog. Here is a gainfully employed, lease-holding man who doesn't crash on friends' couches after being sued for nonpayment of rent.

He asks me to wait in the living room while he cleans the bedroom.

"It's really messy," he says. "I'd hate for you to see it like that."

"Whatever it is, it's nothing compared to what you saw at my place."

"Just hang on. It'll only be a minute."

He rustles in the room behind the closed door. My phone rings. Nathan. I pick up, say nothing.

"They do a terrible job in there," he announces to my silence. "I'm already out."

The line goes dead. I rap on the bedroom door.

"Hey . . . hiding bodies in there?"

"Just a minute! It's really, really messy."

"Nathan just called, and he's out."

The Helicopter Pilot opens the door to a tidy room. He loans me some of his old capoeira clothes to sleep in, washes the gel out of his meticulously styled short black hair, and climbs into bed. I get in beside him, and we fall asleep. A few hours later, I rise, thank him, and head to Family Court. Scrolling through emails while waiting in line, I find messages from other friends who heard from Nathan the night before.

I send a message to Nathan's parents, explaining what happened.

I wait all day in court. Everyone else here has it worse. A little girl complains to a caseworker of a man who tried to shoot her mother's boyfriend. A woman in dark lipliner and sweatpants paces the room. "They don't even know these kids," she shouts over and over. An Asian man pleads with his teenage daughter, who sits facing away from him, arms folded across her chest: "I need to see you! Please, let me see you!" Guards keep watch. My tragedy is small in comparison. I am fortunate, a fortunate maker of bad decisions. A man shouts "goddamn it" while exiting the chambers of the Honorable Lee Hand Elkins. This is a good name for a character in a Southern Gothic novel. Hand. And speaking of hands, Nathan has forced his own. With the restraining order following The Destruction, he will be barred from the very place he refused to leave.

I am called before the Honorable L.H.E., who reviews the incident reports placed in front of him. I play the voicemails on speaker. He grants the order of protection. "This guy broke all your things, and I would not want the next thing he breaks to be you," he says.

Late in the afternoon, in another waiting room where the clerk will call me up to retrieve my order of protection paperwork, I call The Profiler.

"Okay, Mom. So you were on to something about 'that Nathan.'"

"Are you okay?"

"You're not going to like what I'm about to tell you, but I really need your support."

I run down the events leading to the restraining order.

"I knew it," she says. "I never liked him. I told you, he's apathetic, unmotivated, and pompous."

"I don't know, what he just did was pretty motivated."

"I make snap judgments about people for a living. I'm an expert. I warned you. See what happens when you don't listen? He lies to you, and now this."

I picture her sitting behind her big desk at the embassy, coffee mug in front of her, surrounded by the many framed awards she'd won during her State Department career and photographs of her with heads of state, celebrities, and me—the two of us in front of the Sphinx, the Venice canals, the Oracle of Delphi . . .

"You're like my Oracle of Bad Boyfriends."

"Things are replaceable," she says. "I'm just glad you're okay."

Something in me shifts. Her sense about Nathan and reaction to The Destruction transcend the irksome deporter-of-boyfriends she's been in the past. She's driven me nuts, but she's been right all along, and incredibly she's showing some empathy. I don't tell her this, though. I can already hear her speaking her trademark phrase, "I was riiii-iight!"

The sky is dark and the wind high that night, rustling the branches of trees with newly green leaves along St. Marks Avenue. The Helicopter Pilot texts to check in. He's been busy working. I thank him, tell him I'm doing all right. Emir arrives and tries to salvage my papers with a hair dryer. We create a Tumblr account to preserve the voicemails for posterity: http://shoesonfire.tumblr.com. They're actually pretty hilarious.

APPLE STORE SYMPATHY—noun 1. The genuine comfort received from Apple Store employees in blue iPad T-shirts when explaining fate of Apple products submerged in bathtub by ex-boyfriend.

"That's gotta be the worst one I've ever heard," the Genius Bar guy says. "And we see a lot of things like that in here. Mostly phones."

"I should interview Apple Store employees about breakup destruction of electronics."

"I have plenty of stories," he says. "But this is the worst."

They cannot save my computers, but it turns out one of my students can.

There's one lanky, bright, friendly kid in my class this semester I'm consistently irritated with. He's gifted at critical thinking and writing. He has so much potential, yet is always full of excuses. Every week, this kid has a reason to miss class: he's going to San Francisco, he's going to Tennessee. What a punk, I think, especially since when he does hand in his assignments, they are A-plus work. While lamenting about my destroyed computers ("A flood in my apartment," I say, not a total lie) to a female student who visits office hours, she asks me why I don't ask Chris for help.

"Why would Chris be able to help? The Apple Store couldn't do it."

"You don't know who Chris is?"

It's a silver lining situation: Chris is Christopher Poole, a.k.a. Moot, the founder of 4chan, the internet relic that spawned prehistoric memes like lolcats and Rickrolling. The "kid" is an online entrepreneur, and he was in San Francisco for meetings at Facebook. He went to Tennessee as a star witness in the Sarah Palin hacker trial. I love that he was there (or not there) in my classroom for months and I had no idea who he really was. (Typical.)

I give Chris the laptops. Two days later, he hands me an external hard drive with most of my files on it. I am so relieved. I tell him he's my hero. We say we'll stay in touch, but soon he leaves the university and I have no way to contact him. "Moot was actually in your class?" people ask. I'd had no idea an internet legend had been sitting right there, in the back row, that his reasons for turning papers in late weren't average student procrastination. It leads me to believe maybe I am still on the right path, maybe there is a reason even for this. Of all the composition classes Moot could have been assigned to, he walked into mine. At the very least it is a cool coincidence that reminds me I do not believe in coincidence.

WHEN I SEE Nathan at another Family Court appointment, he is impeccably dressed in a new suit and glasses, looking like the type who might even be approved by The Profiler. He reaches for something in his pocket. He has an iPhone! I suspect it's all been purchased with the stolen euros. I have a response from his parents, "Doesn't sound good. Thanks for letting us know. M&C." That's it. They're taking his side.

Nathan and I stand before a red-lipsticked Judge Judy clone in the courtroom. I mention the stolen euros, but without tangible proof there is nothing Judge Judy can do about it. Nathan turned a profit from The Destruction. Judge Judy advises me to keep the order of protection current while I sue Nathan in Civil Court. More court? Family Court can keep Nathan away, Judge Judy's twin says, but to try for actual compensation, I will need to bring a civil suit against him.

"I need to get my stuff from the apartment," Nathan says.

"What possessions?" Judge Judy asks.

"Books, clothes, waffle iron . . . "

"Oh, man CANNOT LIVE without his waffle iron," she says, and the courtroom ripples with scattered laughter. I wonder if she's aware of her Judy resemblance, purposefully hamming it up. It's the one redemptive moment in an otherwise frustrating process.

Two police officers accompany Nathan to the apartment, where, under my supervision, he takes the waffle iron away. It's not much as far as retribution for The Destruction, but I have a Buddhist tendency to believe in forgiveness, not revenge.

THE HELICOPTER PILOT suggests I fight out my feelings—well, dance-fight—by joining him for a capoeira class his friend is teaching at a gym on the outskirts of Philly. As soon as we set foot in the room, he starts doing backflips and hands-free cartwheels. I'm impressed. I can't get the basic move, *ginga* (pronounced "jinga" and translating to "swing"), down, but the class is exhilarating, the best workout.

The Helicopter Pilot watches me fumble as I attempt to mimic the guy in front of me.

"Get out of your head," he says. "This is natural movement. Don't copy him."

I leave the gym on a natural high, mesmerized by capoeira and The Helicopter Pilot. On the road trip back to the city, I decide to sign up for capoeira classes at the academy up the street from my apartment. Not only is it an optimal outlet for my post-Nathan anger, but if I dedicate myself to learning it, The Helicopter Pilot and I can play together. (Capoeira, The Helicopter Pilot explains, is referred to, technically, as a "game," and capoeiristas are its "players.")

Back in Brooklyn, I climb the flight of stairs to the capoeira academy and sign up for the beginner series. Classes start June 1. It's early May. I'll have to train more with The Helicopter Pilot in the meantime.

There's one problem. He stops calling.

At first I figure he's busy, but days pass, and after a full week I get the sinking suspicion that it's intentional. I know from lurking on his page that he's still posting about his activities on Facebook: a particularly challenging session of parkour, Bikram yoga class, pictures of the view from his helicopter.

And then: "I'm in love with the girl who brought me toasted almond ice cream pops."

Unless I've suddenly become an amnesiac, Our Lady of the Toasted Almond Ice Cream Pops isn't me. He's broken it off in a status update.

"You're great," he says when I call to confront him. "But I realized the feelings I thought I should be having for you, I was having for her."

"What does that even mean?"

"It's just that your life seems . . . complicated. And with her it's easier."

"Easy? You want something easy? Good luck with that."

So that's what he was doing in his room that night: hiding her stuff. I picture him stuffing bras and panties and her yoga pants and the cute pictures of them she had framed for his nightstand into the closet. I contemplate asking for a refund for the capoeira lessons but decide not to. I can dance-fight my way back from all this. I'll become disciplined and centered. Instead of something I do for or with some guy, it will be something I do for me.

"I told you," says The Profiler. "That helicopter pilot wasn't right for you. Those guys tend to be objective, scientific, and practical. I can't say pilots wouldn't be interested in the arts, but they meet so many people and travel so much, they may have roving eyes. He's interested in science and mechanics. He's in such a different world than yours. A pilot's background and experience don't mesh with your literary and humanistic interests. A scientist doing research on genes—I have a more positive feeling toward that, because there's more questioning of the universe. A pilot just seems extremely . . . practical."

"Okay, I get it," I say. "We didn't date for that long. We didn't even have sex."

I DON'T SEE The Helicopter Pilot again. It's as if he just got in his helicopter and flew out as quickly as he flew in. As if he simply had been there to airlift me out of the circle of fire.

AFTER A MEDIATION meeting in Civil Court that ends with Nathan officially owing six thousand dollars in damages, to be paid in monthly installments, we speak directly for the first time since the night of The Destruction. The mediator is so good at her job that she neutralizes the mood between us. It's neither amicable nor hostile.

"Are you going to try for shared custody of Baxter?" I ask.

"Wouldn't be a good idea," Nathan says. "My therapist says I need distance."

He apologizes for what he's done. On the way to the subway, we stop at Starbucks and he buys me a latte (gasp!), though he still denies stealing the euros. He afforded to stay at the Jane Hotel in the West Village and buy new clothes and electronics with the money his parents wired, he says.

"Why are his parents such enablers?" I wonder to The Profiler on the phone.

"You always take your child's side," she says.

A few months later, Nathan's monthly checks start arriving. Though I only ultimately receive half the promised settlement, I don't go after him for the remaining three thousand. It's worth more to me to leave it all behind.

Two years later, walking Baxter around the neighborhood, I see him at a sidewalk table at the corner bar, exhaling a cloud of smoke. My heart races. I turn up the avenue and speed-walk the other way, not glancing back. Another night, he sits on the stoop of a brownstone. He's back in the neighborhood. Will I see him in the café where I write? The grocery store? The bar where I meet friends for happy hour? Why am I afraid to run into him, I wonder, when if anyone should feel shame it is he? Next time, I will face him. I don't need to run away or be ashamed. I can ask how he's doing, about the money he still owes. Every evening on my walk home from capoeira class I expect to run into him. I rehearse for our confrontation. Only a very New York thing happens: somebody moves to your neighborhood and you never see him again.

BRAZILIAN FIGHT CLUB, A.K.A. "FOREIGN EXERCISE CLASS"

I WANT MY MOTHER to want to watch my capoeira class the way a four-year-old basks in her mom's enthusiasm for gymnastics or a dance recital—looking on from the sidelines, beaming and clapping. But I am not a four-year-old. I have crossed the threshold of thirty, and though my mother enthusiastically observes me when it comes to dating, she does not want to watch my capoeira class. The single place where I actually want her eyes on my every move is the one place she won't scrutinize. "I like it when you do a reading after you write something," she says. "I'll come to those." Capoeira is physical, therefore not intellectual, or so she believes. But out of everything I've ever studied or attempted, capoeira has taught me the most valuable lesson,[4] a kind of soulful independence—from a man, from my mother—that has complicated, challenged, and also deepened my quest for the right partnership.

When my mother visits, some version of this conversation ensues:

"Hey, Mom, it's almost time for capoeira. Will you come?"

"Still going to your foreign exercise class?"

"It's not an 'exercise class.'"

---

[4] Let's get the cultiness thing out of the way: I understand how people can think of capoeira as a "cult"— yeah, it's kinda culty in that people who really take to it band together and become obsessed. Those who walk through the doors of Raizes do Brasil Academy fall into two camps: the "I don't get its" who never come back, and the "This is the most fun and incredible thing I've ever dones" who can't stay away. But it's not a cult. Though capoeira has connections with *candomble*, modern capoeira *regional*—the fighting style we practice—adheres to no religious tradition. While some can't help but revere their *mestre*—there's a funny *Bob's Burgers* episode about this called "Sexy Dance Fighting" that you should watch a clip of on YouTube—there's no after-class Kool-Aid, maybe just a beer at the bar down the street. Still, when we played in Prospect Park, people confused us with Hare Krishnas or something because of the music and all-white uniforms.

"I think I'll clean the house and walk Baxter."

Revision to previous statement:

My mother would rather pick up dog poop and sweep dust bunnies than watch me play capoeira. Occasionally, I am successful at dragging her to class. "Promise we'll leave as soon as it's over," she says, plunking down on the bench at the front of the room.

She takes out her iPhone. Excited to have some evidence of my ever so slightly increasing skill level, I bound over, sweaty and excited:

"Did you see that *beija flor*?[5] Did you film it?"

"What? I'm reading Facebook. So many interesting things on my newsfeed."

"But . . . I was *defying gravity*, Mom!"

"I did take photos and videos of you the other year." Her eyes dart back to her screen. "Let's go to that new Italian place around the corner when you're finished. It has excellent reviews on TripAdvisor—"

Dismayed, I return to the *roda* (pronounced "ho-da," the circle inside which capoeira is played, originally designed to hide players from outside eyes). I revel in the irony that in the one place I wish my mother would pay more attention, the thing that interests me most is, to her, the least interesting thing about me.

I WISH I could say I started for myself, but as with many things, I did it because of a guy. The Helicopter Pilot, formerly a professional capoeirista, had to take me all the way to Philadelphia to get me interested in the Afro-Brazilian martial art that was taught at an academy half a block from my Brooklyn apartment. For three years, I emerged daily from the subway to the call-and-response singing in Portuguese pouring from the academy's windows. I enjoyed hearing the beat of the *atabaque* (drum) and tones of the *berimbau*—an instrument made of a steel string, a wooden bow, and a gourd. But until I dated The Helicopter Pilot, it didn't occur to me to try the class.

---

5 "Hummingbird"—a fast, acrobatic arm balance.

I'm not naturally athletic or physically gifted—I regularly trip on the sidewalk—but suddenly, I could not have been more intrigued. This was how I acted with men. If they were interested in something, so was I. I wanted it to go both ways, too: I'd once imagined a partner as the one person I would enjoy doing everything with, and when things didn't pan out that way, I'd be devastated. When I took my ex-husband to Vanessa Redgrave's one-woman adaptation of Joan Didion's *The Year of Magical Thinking* (about, ironically, losing her husband), he said, "Never again will I spend two hours listening to some lady in an Adirondack chair." When I got a graduate school rejection, he called it "a relief": tuition was expensive and a writing degree, useless. Clearly, our values were different. He was followed by his polar opposite: Nathan, not The Gentle Poet I imagined him to be. The next guy literally swooped down from the sky, briefly, as if to save me. A helicopter pilot and capoeirista—who wouldn't be enticed?

In the class he invited me to, I mixed up the most basic movements, which involved feats of physical coordination. How did people do this? I later visited the second-floor studio up the street from my apartment to find out. It smelled of fried chicken from the Spanish diner downstairs. The students wore white uniforms, pants held up by tasseled cords of various colors. I signed up for the four-week "absolute-beginner series," imagining the pilot tutoring me—right up until the day he ended it in a status update.

I had finished grad school, was on my own for the first time in a decade, and suddenly found myself with more time on my hands. I liked capoeira. I may have started because of a guy, but I wasn't going to quit because of him, too.

THE CLASSES AT Raizes do Brasil Academy in Brooklyn were held in an open room with a hardwood floor and mirrored wall. Students faced the mirror, dressed in capoeira T-shirts emblazoned with the school logo, the berimbau, and a Brazilian flag. Mestre Foca, the tanned, muscular Brazilian codirector whose nickname means "seal," told us everyone in capoeira gets an *apelido* (nickname) eventually. This tradition began when capoeira was illegal in Brazil (until 1937), to obscure players' identities, so that if caught by police, they could not reveal fellow capoeiristas' identities even under torture. The *apelido* can be an animal you resemble, something about your profession, or another characteristic. A postal worker was Messagero (messenger); a visiting capoeirista from the sister academy in California had a shaved head, hence, Melão (melon). Under Foca's tutelage, I got ginga down. Next came basic kicks, dodges, and cartwheels.

The main event comes toward the end of class—the fifteen to twenty minutes of the roda, in which capoeira is played—improvised—by two people at a time in the center of the circle. Though it appears to be some combination of fight and dance, we were taught that capoeira is a game. It combines kicks, dodges, and *floreios* (acrobatics). For beginners, that's cartwheels. The attacks and dodges during the roda and the constant switching of players mirrored a relationship: dance, fight, and game all at once.

One day, Mestre Foca started calling me Joaninha—Portuguese for "ladybug." He didn't say why. It made sense on a literal level as I'm small, or maybe he thought I was lucky. I've always had a thing for ladybugs—spotting them, having them land on me, wishing on them. I loved the name so much that three months after my first *batizado*—an advancement ceremony where I got a half-yellow cord—I got little ladybugs tattooed on the back of my neck. I thought of how ladybugs' wings are hidden until they spread them and fly. I began to feel that I was finding my own.

Foca's wife, a blond, blue-eyed badass with a twelve-pack who grew up in Africa, was known as Instrutora Rouxinol—Instructor Nightingale. The day she forced me to do a handstand against the wall changed my life, or at least my perspective on what was possible. (For ten years of yoga, I "didn't do" inversions.) I looked at the people doing headstands and handstands as freaky athletes, convinced that that could never be me. "The wall is there, Joaninha," Rouxinol said. "What are you afraid of?"

Maybe it's just about taking time to be playful, but I swear there's something about being upside-down—all the blood to the head?—that's a natural mood booster. My suspicions were confirmed by a UCLA study that followed mildly depressed participants who began doing inversions (as part of a yoga practice) twice a week for five weeks. Subjects reported "significant decreases in self-reported symptoms of depression and trait anxiety." Given that capoeira is yoga-plus, with its headstands, handstands, bridges, cartwheels, and walkovers, it is not a stretch (sorry) to imagine that it would have the same effect. We'd have a less tense society if adults did handstands every day.

At first I treated capoeira like the gym—arriving just on time to stretch quietly, then, as soon as class ended, grabbing my stuff from the cubby and rushing out. This was conditioning as a New Yorker. After a few months, though, I noticed people sprawled out on the floor in the entry area outside the studio after class, talking about significant others, family members, career moves. Once I emerged from my post–Helicopter Pilot pity party and became more present, I realized these capoeira people knew everything about one another. I wondered if they'd all been friends who signed up for capoeira together and motivated one another to attend classes that made bench-pressing a rhino seem easy. (I once had to run around the room with a two-hundred-pound man on my back as part of the warm-up.) It turned out to be the other way around: they met there.

This martial art from Brazil had turned a bunch of Brooklyn neighbor-strangers into a tight-knit group. They weren't just in a "foreign exercise class"—they were a community. Capoeira, it hit me like a *martelo* to the head, is ultimately about connecting with people. It made sense. Capoeira is all about the relationship of self to others. When I told my mother about my new hobby and its social potential, she disagreed.

"You won't meet worthwhile men in that exercise class. If you want to do something cultural, why not go to lectures at the 92nd street Y or at museums? Or wine-tasting classes? The men at those—"

"I'm learning capoeira for myself, Mom. It's the one place where I'm purposefully barring myself from the idea or potential of 'meeting someone,' at least in the way you're talking about. I won't date anyone from capoeira. It's one of my few personal rules. I'd never want anything to ruin it or make it awkward to go there four to six days a week."

"Well if you're spending that much of your free time there, how are you ever going to meet someone?"

"I guess I'll end up old and alone doing handstands against the wall at the retirement home."

"I don't appreciate your sarcasm. This is serious. You're thirty now. How much longer are you going to do this?"

But I was obsessed. Capoeira was so challenging I couldn't stop. I had to prove to myself that trying to do what felt impossible would be worth it even if I failed. I struggled with the choreographed sequences. In the beginning, entering the roda at all was a victory. "Buying in" is voluntary. You have to make yourself play. The only other option is to be the one who doesn't. The roda is also a lot like love: you risk getting hurt every time but take the chance for the exhilaration of the game.

Capoeira was becoming a different source of strength. At first I thought it changed me, but later I realized it showed me the independent spirit I'd had inside all along: When my ex-husband didn't approve of graduate school, I reapplied for the following year, got in, and went. After the poet lied about arranging a trip to the Keys for my thirtieth birthday, I went on my own. But only after starting capoeira did I consciously stop seeing a romantic relationship as my utmost need. When I started dating someone, I didn't feel the need for instantaneous exclusivity. He wasn't automatically my one and only. I was channeling my urge for commitment into capoeira.

When things got tough in the roda, Foca would say, "Volta ao mundo," meaning "around the world." When players collide, get tired, or need to calm down during the game, they can stop playing and walk around the inside perimeter of the roda. It's a metaphor for taking a moment. "When life is hard, when your boss yells at you, when you fight with your husband or wife, remember volta ao mundo," he told us.

I had to volta ao mundo about the capoeira academy itself when things changed suddenly. A year and a half into my training, Foca and Rouxinol announced they were moving away in two weeks and closing the academy. Everybody panicked, writing on one another's Facebook walls: "What am I going to do with myself?" and "We're going to need a support group." Thankfully, a young instructor from Brazil took over and reopened the school in a tucked-away space in Gowanus, a twenty-minute bike ride away, which I took in all weather. Unexpected change is sometimes inevitable. Still, my journey continued without my first teachers. The beginners helped rebuild the community—doing street performances, handing out flyers, decorating the space, and attending every class, sometimes two in a row.

In New York City, a place where neighbors pass each other by without speaking, I became close with people I otherwise would have sat across from on the subway platform but never would have interacted with: Mulher Gato, a twenty-three-year-old prodigy who was already a lawyer; Barbie, a pretty blond kickboxer and food connoisseur with a masters in sociology (when Foca gave her the apelido Baaaahhh-beh, she asked, "Oh, what does that mean in Portuguese? Like, 'kickass warrior woman'?" "Não . . . Bahhhh-beh . . . like the doll," he responded, to her dismay); and Pinguinha, which means "penguin," a deceptive apelido for a sharp, sexy, multilingual CFO who can MacGyver any problem away. After classes, we all went out regularly for sushi or a glass of wine or two or three. Some weekends we went dancing at a Brazilian club in Brooklyn. We laughed about everything. I felt happier and more in love with these women than I had with any of my exes (except Emir, who didn't technically count as an ex, and who occasionally joined us).

At my second batizado I received a full-yellow cord from Profesor Curu, the new teacher, meaning that I was still a beginner but with a foundation. I invited my mother and she came to watch, one of the first times I had that feeling of actually wanting my mother's eyes on me. (Though when I invited her to subsequent batizados, she always said,

"I've already been to one, why do I need to go again?" To which I sniffled and my teenage self surfaced as I countered with, "But I've gotten better, don't you want to see?")

Even in a right long-term relationship, the honeymoon period wears off, but you figure out how to stay committed.

"What should I do to get better at capoeira?" I asked one of my favorite teachers, expecting an answer about cross-training, yoga, or swimming.

"More capoeira," he said.

It's been more challenging and satisfying than my former sport of trying to force those guys-of-the-moment to be the one. The same forcefulness that served me well in other areas—sticking with capoeira was one—had been a fatal flaw in love.

My mother still doesn't connect how capoeira lessons are applicable outside the academy, how bridge rolls and hammer kicks might translate into a sharper mind or more successful life, but I hope to convince her, if not of this, at least to take a video the day I'm able to finally execute a successful *macaco*.[6]

"You seem centered since you started capoeira," a pre-capoeira friend told me. I agreed, though sometimes I still imagined "resolving things" with The Helicopter Pilot in the roda, perhaps with a swift martelo to the head. But not really. I should thank him, because without him, I wouldn't have traveled, two years into my training, to Rio and Brasilia with Barbie and Pinguinha. I wouldn't have had the pleasure of observing the Brazilian capoeira batizado tradition in which big muscled men throw straight kicks and right hooks (in Brazil they do not fuck around) in the roda and then give twenty-minute speeches about what capoeira has meant in their lives and how proud they are of one another, during which they choke up and cry.[7] ("A memoir about this trip would be called *Fight, Talk, Cry*," we joked.) I wouldn't have found the aspect

---

6 "Monkey"—a backflip from the ground.
7 Yes, I still promise it's not a cult.

of capoeira that's Profiler-approved, even if she won't admit it: an international network of cultural exchange—capoeiristas welcome and house each other the world over. I wouldn't be sitting in this café across from Lake Merritt in Oakland, peering enviously through the window at the energetic street roda I walked away from to finish writing my capoeira story. I wouldn't have realized that men who weren't right for me could still point me to great things. I wouldn't have discovered that the art that comes as close as possible to teaching people to fly—that uplifted me and sent me to places I couldn't have imagined I would go—is still the very thing that grounds me.

THE GOLD STAR
BREAKUP

"**A**NDY'S HAVING A party tomorrow night," Emir said, scrolling through his phone on the Megabus ride from New York to Boston.

"Who's Andy?" I asked.

"You don't know Andy? Everyone knows Andy."

I didn't, and I was barely listening anyway since I'd originally planned to skip the ten-year college reunion. It came on the heels of a particularly disastrous breakup (The Destruction by Nathan). Subjecting myself to a bunch of successful married people with kids for a weekend of "fun activities" like a boat cruise and karaoke night sounded painful. Emir sweet-talked me into it: We'd been "together" since college. I could be his date. His partner was staying home. Maybe I'd find a reunion hookup. That would be good for me, Emir said. "I don't want to tell you what to do," he continued, "but you're one of those people who is never single." It would make me feel better, he insisted, and it would be fun. I told Emir I'd go, but he had to promise he would not abandon me for one second with those happily married classmates.

When we arrived at the first event, a boat cruise around the Boston Harbor, I understood why Emir had been surprised I'd never met Andy. Andy required no profiling because you immediately knew him. He was one of those Robin Williams–esque charismatic types. Theatrical, attention-drawing nature. Center of gravity of any room he walks into. He was his own small planet, pulling people into his orbit. And I was an eager satellite from the moment Emir introduced us.

With his wingtip Doc Martens, pinstriped suit pants, and wallet chain, Andy looked as if he'd stepped out of a time machine from that moment in the late '90s when swing dancing became briefly popular again. He had a shaved head and a Fu Manchu mustache he named Fred. Emir hadn't been exaggerating. Everyone did know Andy. He greeted them all with cheers and hugs. During our first conversation, we figured out he must have sold me late-night pizza at the campus convenience store in college, though neither of us could recall a specific instance.

At otherwise awkward reunion karaoke, Andy belted James's "Laid" like a professional rock star. I wondered why he didn't have a wife or girlfriend by his side. He told me he was divorced from his college sweetheart who hadn't gone to our college. Outside the karaoke venue, we bonded over being young divorcées, married in our early twenties and divorced before our third decade.

"My ex-wife got remarried fast," he said. "I'm that guy in the crappy rom-com *Two Buck Chuck*, where every woman goes on to find the love of her life right after him."

We laughed.

"I was born with bad luck," he said. "If something bad can happen, it happens to me."

"I don't believe it," I said.

The rest of the night, we talked nonstop. He'd studied advertising instead of majoring in film out of pressure to be practical and conventional, though he also liked aspects of being an ad major—he had a natural knack for slogans. He's the only person I've met who had his own: Embrace Your Awesome. It was the motivation behind everything he did, he said, coming from a conservative family that operated under a "what-would-the-neighbors-think" mentality. I could relate. While The Profiler wouldn't have cared what the neighbors thought, as a Foreign Service family we were supposed to represent our country 24/7 overseas. Andy was bold and loud and different, the self-proclaimed proverbial black sheep. Growing up, he'd been embarrassed, but after his divorce he decided to embrace it, call it awesome instead.

Like me, Andy was an obsessive recorder of moments, a documentarian. I had no idea what I was getting into when accepting his Facebook request. He kept a photo-diary there, a series of albums called What I Saw Today.

He relayed his philosophy about this in one post:

Moments.

There's so many of 'em. Hard to keep track sometimes. Which ones should I care about? Which ones can I forget?

It doesn't matter which moments you choose. As long as you regularly take some time to stop and appreciate a thing as it is happening . . . even if it's something silly.

Document the moment. Make it holy. With a camera, with a sketch, with a poem, or just simply making sure you've committed it to memory.

Enjoy then forever.

(I assumed he meant to write "enjoy *them* forever," but I liked the ring of "enjoy then forever," which sounded appropriately Yoda-esque.)

Andy must have enjoyed all the moments, because he took pictures of each one: a rain puddle, scrawled graffiti in the bathroom, a loaf of bread, a person he'd met for five minutes. He saw the world through myths and stories. He often quoted the novel *The Last Unicorn* ("There are no happy endings because nothing ends"), but the Chinese legend of Dragon's Gate was Andy's number one go-to tale. No one who met him walked away without hearing it.

Dragon's Gate is located at the top of a waterfall. Carp swim upstream toward it, against the current. Many dangers await along the way: hungry eagles and bears, fishermen's lines. Most never make it. But one little carp, yearning for something beyond the pond, dared swim upstream against all advice. He fought his mortal terrors, tricked the dragon guarding the gate into flying away, and plunged through, transformed—by courage, dedication, and persistence—into a dragon himself.

Andy told me about the sleeve tattoo he was getting, in stages, representing the legend. He felt stuck in his administrative job at a neuroscience laboratory and dreamed of being a filmmaker. He only allowed himself to get parts of the tattoo as he took steps toward accomplishing his goal.

IN THE DORM suite where I was staying, we kissed as lightning flashed over the Boston Common. Nature's fireworks. The next night, he picked me up for his party in his Toyota Corolla, named Clarence. Glowing Christmas lights lined its interior, something I already suspected was "very Andy." At the party, he invited all the guests to decorate the walls of his room with blacklight paint. *How appropriate for a college throwback party*, I thought. Andy called our amateur scribblings "art."

That night, after the guests cleared out, he came back to the dorm suite where Emir and I were staying (in separate bedrooms). In the morning, we went across the street to Starbucks, he kissed me goodbye on the sidewalk, and I was sure I wouldn't see him again. Andy was only supposed to be a reunion hookup, maybe a friend to see when he happened to be in New York or I in Boston. We certainly weren't going to impact the rest of each other's lives. But Andy kept texting. I accepted his proposal that he come visit me in Brooklyn the following weekend. For two days, we left the apartment only for food and coffee, and to buy a razor when I convinced him to shave off Fred, that he'd look better without it. I also tried to get him to stop wearing his keys clipped to his belt. That was a battle I lost. He gave me a clip of my own instead, and I discovered the joys of not digging through a bag for keys.

I wasn't looking for a relationship and neither was he, but soon we found ourselves trading weekends between New York and Boston. He drove Clarence—no longer strung with Christmas lights since a cop pulled him over and told him to take them down. I took Amtrak or the Chinatown bus. We didn't commit. We were just having fun. I wrote and trained capoeira and went on some lackluster dates. I was trying something that felt unnatural for me, the open relationship. I told myself I was in it for the regular, safe sex, which was kinky and fun—he gave me toys and stripper heels and handcuffs (I'd already been curious about light BDSM, but I hadn't found a partner who would want to experiment).

To my mother's horror, Andy helped me rediscover a punk rock side I'd long abandoned. His roommate, who had just finished her apprenticeship with the master who was inking scenes from Dragon's Gate onto the canvas of Andy's skin, covered a tattoo my ex-husband designed with a nine-blossomed lotus mandala that symbolizes strength, completion, and wholeness in one's self. I returned for spontaneous tattoos—the ladybugs on the back of my neck and the beginnings of a half sleeve of winding purple Lisianthus flowers I'd dreamed were winding up my arm.

The changes in my appearance continued: while visiting him in Boston for a weekend, I went to a South End salon and had my hair bleached out and dyed fire engine red. After Thai food and lychee martinis in Williamsburg during one of Andy's New York weekends, we dropped into a piercing place and I got a stud in my nose. These were things I'd never imagined doing in my thirties, but Andy was helping me see less conventionally too. I was still subconsciously trying to please my mother, and who was I? Being with Andy freed my sense of play. He called himself a healer. Coming from someone else's mouth it would have sounded pretentious, but Andy was sincere. He had a particular way of inspiring people to do what they really wanted, even though he struggled with it himself, toggling between playing it safe and leaving it all behind to take a risk toward the less secure path of becoming a filmmaker. He was responsible before he was reckless.

Andy and I were taking it slow, keeping our options open. I wasn't fully certain. Neither was he. We decided to see what would happen given time and no forced parameters for the relationship. I went on some dates. I adored a book editor who stopped calling after we had sex. I attended a friend's wedding with a guy who didn't want to use a condom. I yelled at him, dressed quickly, and left the room. I went to Italy with a man who told me he couldn't really be into me because he didn't like my teeth. I called Andy from a phone booth at four in the morning. I missed him. Andy wouldn't criticize my teeth. He wouldn't criticize anyone's teeth. He'd tell us all our teeth were awesome.

He couldn't wait to see me when I got back, he said. What was I doing in Italy with this guy who didn't even want me when Andy was dogsitting and sending romantic emails? For someone who wanted an open relationship, he was acting a lot like a partner. I started treating him like one.

By October, Andy and I were exclusive. I was his date for the wedding of two of his close friends on a bucolic farm in Vermont.

"Looked like a great wedding," my mother said after seeing a picture on Facebook. "I wouldn't say the same about your date."

"What? You've never even met him."

"I don't like what he posts on Facebook."

"What don't you like about it?"

"He's made himself into a character," she said.

"He *is* a character. That's just him. You've never even had one conversation with him."

"He's not a bad person," she said. "He's just not right for you."

"I'm not claiming that he is." And then, in true Andy spirit, "But you're being unnecessarily negative. You need to let other people embrace who they are."

My mother was profiling Andy based on, well, his profile: a half-sleeve tattoo and status updates that tended to go along the lines of, "The Moby show RAWKED." There was nothing that could fully represent who he was—the man who loved children and the ocean as much as I did, who was talented at baking and home repair. Though she'd been right before, I hadn't asked for her professional evaluation. I wasn't looking to get married, but I was open to what might evolve between us. I didn't want her input, at least not yet. I wanted to get to know him, let our story unfold. What I knew for sure: he was strong, a multitasker, and a leader. He was "most likely to be famous" in his high school yearbook.

"You should date the neuroscientist," my mother said, "not the lab administrator."

"That's not profiling, it's snobbery," I argued. "I should date the guy who I have fun and connect with, who treats me well and loves me for who I am."

The Profiler and I were still at odds in how we approached the whole "how you know who's right for you" question. She had her pragmatic criteria, and I, my often too forgiving inclination to take chances. But I didn't want to online-date or meet men my mother would try to fix me up with. I wanted the story. With Andy, I thought, *Here's the kind of story I'm looking for.* A romantic "how we met" story. The partners who went to college together but hadn't known each other in college. Soul mates that started out as a reunion hookup. Great loves who took a long time to realize they were right for each other after all.

THE FOLLOWING YEAR, after spending his first thirty-three years in Massachusetts, he quit his job to move to Brooklyn and into a new apartment with me. Andy quickly found work as a freelance production assistant and assistant director on shoots around the city and got the next stage of his Dragon's Gate tattoo, water swirling on his chest—the first approach to the falls. He would prove The Profiler wrong. He was already succeeding. But he pointed out that these, too, were administrative jobs. He feared he was repeating the same patterns, even if in the right industry.

I came home from work to find him watching reruns of *ALF*, the '80s show with the alien puppet. He talked about feeling like an alien himself, an alien meat robot, how he didn't know what it meant to be human. He said he was depressed. When I expressed surprise—I'd never seen him like this, and of course he knew how to be human, he was an excellent human—he confessed he had self-diagnosed as bipolar. If he was, I suspected it was slow cycling. In the time I'd known him, he was joyous, outgoing, and in love with life. Once we lived together, I learned that the high highs came with low lows.

Our relationship was full of ups and downs, too. We clashed in a way we hadn't when we lived in separate cities and saw each other for weekend-long dates. I accused him of forgetfulness, of being mentally elsewhere. "Is something wrong with your brain?" I'd sometimes say in the heat of a fight.

He complained that our apartment building was too "uppity," and I accused him of secretly wanting to live in a Bushwick loft with fifteen aspiring artists in pop-up rooms with canvas sheets for walls, where he could have as much clutter as he wanted around. "No, I want to be here, with you," he recanted.

We argued over his collection and accumulation of camera equipment, tools, and knickknacks. "Better to have it and not need it than need it and not have it," was another of his mantras, and it led to something just short of hoarding.

We had stupid fights over the meaning of art. Another of his trademark sayings was, Art: Where You Find It. I liked this, but he called everything art, just as he had the blacklight paint squiggles we'd decorated his former apartment room with at the reunion. I insisted art was labored over, elevated—not something anyone could throw together in no time or by accident. I knew it was a silly fight, but my jaw clenched anytime he spent forty-five minutes photographing a spray-painted stencil on a lamppost and tagging it "Art."

When I got some rejections for a book I'd been writing for years, Andy secretly taught himself bookmaking and made me a beautiful handmade hardcover of my book for my thirty-first birthday. "This is art!" I told him. I loved the object and the intent, and yet it brought my sadness about the book's rejection to the forefront just as I was starting to move on. The gift made me feel better and worse at the same time— like our relationship, which both energized me and left me depleted, as if

I was synced with his up-and-down cycles. I felt guilt over my ingratitude for Andy's homemade gift.

When he collaborated with a lighting designer at work, he came home and said, "We'll go on the road lighting shows for bands on tour in Europe!"

He feared I was trying to hold him back when I was only trying to hold on to him. Soon, though, he lost touch with the lighting designer. He didn't go to Europe.

There were equally good times. We threw big parties for which Andy would spend two days making his famous eggplant parm. My friends loved him. We went hiking on Bear Mountain on the coldest day of the year and propelled ourselves down snowbanks using our coats as sleds. Somewhere along the line of this tug-of-war between Andy and me, I started wanting a ring. It was more about where we were in life—that place in one's thirties where wedding invitations start arriving by the boatload—than it was about Andy. He couldn't afford one yet, he said when we talked about moving our relationship forward. I wanted the ring and was also relieved when I couldn't have it.

When I planned a trip to Brazil with two of my capoeira girlfriends, Andy and I went "ring shopping" in Chinatown. Having heard from other female capoeira friends that certain Brazilian men would be relentless in pursuit of solo women travelers, I wanted a token to show I was taken (not yet knowing that a ring was no deterrent). We took to this search for my "engagement ring" among fake designer purses and catfish being bludgeoned to death with a bat on the sidewalk with as much care as if we'd been at Cartier or Tiffany's. This one was too big, that one looked too fake, one was shaped like a flower and spanned the width of three fingers.

LONG AFTER THE sun went down, as the shopkeepers of Chinatown began pulling the gates down over their storefronts, I found the right piece of cheap metal and glass, a small and delicate one, one that, almost, if you looked at it from far enough away, could have been real.

THE PROFILER CAME to visit from Madrid for her sixtieth birthday. Andy and I had been living together for five months. It was late November, and a brisk, cold wind droned as we walked through Prospect Park on our way to Song, a Park Slope Thai institution. Andy knew my mother had profiled him and that she hadn't been an immediate fan, unlike everybody else who knew him. He was a warm people person and used to being liked. The Profiler befuddled him. So he had a plan: he was going to pay for dinner. Paying for dinner was the gentlemanly thing to do and would steer her from thinking he didn't make enough money, something she'd picked up on that he found to be both true and hurtful.

As we strolled through the park, Andy told The Profiler about his first film job in New York. Within a week of moving, he had landed a production assistant gig on a major Bollywood movie.

"The star is the Julia Roberts of India," Andy said. "And this is her big comeback role."

"What's the script about?" The Profiler asked.

"An Indian woman in New York who falls for a much younger man, a photographer. We just did some scenes in Central Park. I was on lockdown, keeping pedestrians out of the frame."

"That sounds like an important job," The Profiler said. I cringed. I could read her subtle sarcasm. If Andy did, he didn't react.

"Oh, it is," Andy said. "There are a lot of logistics to it. And people don't generally like to be told where they can and can't walk."

At Song, Andy discovered he'd forgotten his wallet. I tried to sneak him my card, but my mother saw. Nothing got by The Profiler. She told me as soon as he walked out to go to the ATM. (The restaurant was cash only.)

"You shouldn't ever give anyone else your PIN."

"Busted. How did you even see under the table?"

"Does someone who really cares about paying for dinner forget his wallet?" she asked.

"He'll pay me back. It's not that big of a deal. He just forgets things sometimes."

"PARENTS HAVE ALWAYS been crazy about me," Andy said later. "Your mother doesn't like me. She doesn't think I'm good enough for you. I'm not rich enough for you."

I leapt to her defense. "Hey, it's not all about money."

"What's it about, then?"

I knew her profile of him: "He's made himself into a character. He's a mess. Look around your apartment." I would never say those things to Andy. It was hurtful and cruel. I just said I didn't know, that it took her time to warm up to people, that she had trust issues. Those weren't untrue points.

WHEN I GOT back from Brazil, Andy and I drove to Boston to visit his family. We'd been on the road for a while, listening to the radio, when Andy said, "You know, what I really want to do is drive back and forth across the country in a van."

"Why would you want to do that?" I asked.

"Have adventures. Meet people. I'd make a documentary."

"If you want to go on a pilgrimage, why not do the Camino de Santiago or something like that? Get out of the country, see other places in the world."

Oh no, I sounded like my mother. Andy lit a menthol Marlboro. I rolled down the passenger-side window of Clarence and stared at the snowbanks lining the edge of the highway.

WE TRAVELED TO Florida for Andy's close friend's wedding. After the wedding, we flew to Miami for our first vacation together. We were walking on Collins Avenue toward News Café, one of my favorite South Beach restaurants. I was glad to create a new memory of the place, to restore it from the dregs of the old, the last place I drank mojitos with Julian. It was Andy's first time in Miami. I wanted it to be the kind of romantic getaway I was addicted to: a day in the Caribbean waves, sundowners at five, alfresco beachside dinners, and dancing and/or long nights of hot hotel sex. It seemed like it would be until somehow the subject of The Profiler came up.

"She makes me feel emasculated," he said. "She looks down on me. She wants to see you with a guy like your Wall Street ex."

"Trust me, she doesn't want you to be like Julian. She doesn't want anybody to be like Julian."

"She makes me feel like I'm not man enough for you," Andy said. "She wants you to be with 'somebody better.' I hate to say this to you honey, but I really don't like your mother. Your mother is a bad person."

I could complain about my mother for the lifespan of a redwood tree, but I was her daughter. I had license. But hearing someone else speak of her that way, I was suppressing smoke coming out of my nostrils. "What makes a person 'bad'?—I mean, a murderer is 'bad' if you ask me."

"*You* talk about her control issues all the time. *You* talk about her critically all the time."

"She's not a *bad person*. She's been hurt and has trust issues. She just has to get to know you better."

"She'll never think I'm good enough."

"She's impossible to please," I said. "Yes, she can be mean, she makes decisions based on superficial qualities, it's what she does for a living, she's won fucking *prizes* for it—it's a lot of pressure."

Andy's dark mood hung over the meal. The salade niçoise may as well have been a plate of sand. I sucked down my mojito and ordered another. We fell silent. News Café would not be replaced with a better memory, not that night. Why did my mother have to be so judgmental? What was it about Miami? My last romantic getaway here ended with Julian trying to pitch my laptop across a hotel room. This time, Andy and I battled over The Profiler's unfounded judgments. I resolved not to return, at least not on a romantic vacation. The place had bad love juju.

ONE MORNING, AS winter was giving way to spring, the sky over Brooklyn flat and gray, I woke up early with a sinking sensation in my stomach. Something was, as The Profiler would say, off. Then Andy said what I wasn't sure of, or hadn't wanted to admit.

"I think we've reached the end of our road."

It was an apt metaphor, considering.

"I don't think I'm meant to love just one person," he continued, "but to love all beings equally."

"Maybe we're not right for each other," I said, "but can you not pull some hippie crap right now?"

This time I wasn't surprised when The Profiler was right. Even when things were good, I'd never been a hundred percent convinced that Andy was the one. But Andy was right about at least one thing. Since my divorce, I hadn't really been ready for or open to a relationship that could lead to marriage. Hence three years of Nathan. After Andy, I was different. Something in me that was broken had healed.

The next man I get involved with will be my future husband.

"He's a nice person," my mother said when I told her. "But he wasn't right for you."

"He wants to go on some spiritual quest across America."

"Why don't you see these things quickly like I do? You spend years with these people. Nathan was worth two dates, if that. And Andy shouldn't have been moving in."

"I like giving people a chance. Why don't you profile your boyfriends?"

"I do."

"And you don't have any boyfriends."

AS SOON AS we broke up, Fred the mustache was back. I'd kept him at bay for nearly two years, when what he'd really needed was to grow wild and free. Andy and Fred and I stayed on good terms as they moved out, made new friends, and kept freelancing on film sets. We accepted that we wanted different—neatly opposed, even—things. He kept me apprised of his "awesome" new life.

"I wish I could have taken you to the zombie march," he wrote.

"And here is a concrete example of why it didn't work," I joked. "I'd rather scoop out my eyeballs with a dull spoon than walk around New York City in red face paint and some old rags pretending to be undead."

In his What I Saw Today albums, I realized our incompatibilities anew, and clearer than ever. There's a picture of him shortly after we broke up, at the Coney Island mermaid parade. He's in neon face paint, dancing at a Moby show after-party. "This is my Valhalla," he posted.

I hate crowds. I longed for a gentle, retiring kind of solitude, and he thrived at massive Events with a capital E. Satisfied with the adventures I'd had traveling and being young, I sought to create my own quirky version of "settling down." Andy, on the other hand, was looking to reclaim some unlived part of his youth, attending shows with mosh pits and gatherings where people pelted each other with pillows and water guns—Pillow Fight Day and Water Fight Day. But I also loved getting to glimpse the world though his childlike sense of wonder.

The best thing about breaking up because you want different things is it allows for a genuinely amicable parting. Andy and I kept in touch and both happily referred to him as "the good ex." We respected our relationship even though it was over, something I hadn't experienced in the past. (Except with Emir, but again, that was a whole different marriage genre.)

"I'm happy I could give you a good breakup," Andy wrote. "You needed that, and I needed an infusion of reckless adventure. Healing each other was grand!"

Though I'd been secretly annoyed when he'd called himself a healer, he was right. Traits that grate your soul in an intimate partner might not even register on the irritation radar in a friendship with the same person.

THE FOLLOWING YEAR, Andy got a gray cargo van, named it Eshe (Egyptian for "home"), and spelled out BURN YOUR STARS BRIGHT on the side in blue painter's tape. On the front bumper he stenciled the Timothy Leary quote FIND THE OTHERS, reversed so people could read it in their rearview mirrors. It became a story Andy made his mission to bring to life. He left to drive back and forth across the country, shooting his own documentary, the first for Embrace Your Awesome Productions, called *Notes to Self*.

"I am going to get Alzheimer's Disease one day," he wrote. "Both my maternal grandmother and grandfather suffered severe dimensia [*sic*], as did my paternal grandfather. While it is not guaranteed, the risk is high . . . and it scares me more than anything. I already have a genetically flawed memory. I watch my father and understand the things he tries to do to mask that this is happening to him even when others in my family get frustrated at his lies. I understand because it's already happening to me . . . I have a very hard time remembering people's names. I often times do not recognize people when I run into them and I see how hurt they are because they think I don't care about them . . . but that's not it. It's my addled brain, my damaged fluff. I am losing my own history because the record in my mind is missing fragments."

Oliver Sacks's case study "The Last Hippie" tells of a young man named Greg who abandoned a more conventional life to become a Hare Krishna: "One problem arose in Greg's second year with the Krishnas—he complained that his vision was growing dim, but this was interpreted, by his swami and others, in a spiritual way: he was 'an illuminate,' they told him. It was his 'inner light' growing. Greg had worried about his eyesight, but was reassured by the swami's spiritual explanation. His sight grew still dimmer, but he offered no further complaints. And indeed, he seemed to be becoming more spiritual by the day—an amazing new serenity had taken hold of him." I wondered about the link between extreme charisma and states of "enlightenment" and mental illness or brain disease. Andy seemed to fit the profile.

He went to Burning Man and never came back.

Andy went from partner to friend to figure I tracked on a screen. My interest in him was renewed with every adventurous moment he posted. He spent his days driving all over the United States, visiting friends and acquaintances along the way, and making new ones. He carried around sheets of gold star stickers, the kind kindergarten teachers give their students for good work or behavior, and handed them out to people he met—from the checkout person at a middle-of-nowhere gas station convenience store to an old woman he rescued from the side of a winding rural road when her car ran out of gas. He made a point of doing random good deeds for strangers. He posted pictures of himself with the people he encountered, with little stories of their encounter and what about them was awesome. Thus they were inducted into his log of members of his Army of Awesome. I was reminded of what Andy had told me about being meant to love all beings equally. I hadn't taken it seriously when he'd said it, but he'd gone and actually done it. He was living "Find the Others," ascending his version of Dragon's Gate Falls, a mishmash of myths. One of the last times I saw him, he gave me a gold star, too. I stuck it on the corner of my phone, but over time it peeled and began to fade away; then I donated the phone to a shelter when a newer version was released.

As I observed the journey Andy chronicled online, I began to wonder what happened to the documentary. Missing "home," he drove to the playa, the desert that in summer briefly houses Burning Man, off-season, and got his van stuck in the mud, where it remained for eighteen days before he could find help digging it out. He posted beautiful photographs of the van in the middle of the Nevada desert on a sunny day—stunning portraits of desert, steel, sky, and the tracks in the earth to where Eshe sat, immobile for the first time since he'd gotten the van.

"Life is best when you live it with reckless abandon and make decisions that do not make logical sense," Andy wrote on Facebook. (Contrary to The Profiler's beliefs, Andy's advice justified all of my past relationships.) Bipolar or not, he'd turned into the polar opposite of the guy who'd worked a day job and played it safe. We'd both been searching for family, "the family you choose," but different types, and we'd found them in different ways. I'd been a passenger in his van before he'd had a van, and where I'd gotten out was a better place. We'd met in an intersection; he was headed deeper into the wildness where I'd paused at a rest stop. On his way out of rational responsibility and on my way toward it, there was this point, this moment, in which we collided before forging on in opposite directions. I watched as his existence became performance art, an online spectacle of glittery nail polish, cartwheels in parking lots, and enormous cutout gold stars he held up atop his van, reflecting the sun.

THE PROFILER VS. THE BY-REFERRAL-ONLY TAROT READER

AN INTERLUDE

"**W**HY DO YOU pay that tarot reader when I can tell you the same things for free?" my mother asks anytime I mention I've brought to my by-referral-only tarot reader my questions and doubts about love. Julian, Nathan, The Helicopter Pilot, Andy—as I've dodged The Profiler, I've paid the by-referral-only tarot reader a hundred dollars to tell me about each man I've been involved with since I was first referred to her by a random painter I met at a gallery opening when I was twenty-three. Love is unpredictable, but if anyone can gain insight into a person, sight unseen, it is this formidable woman with a large presence and purple-streaked bouffant. On the top floor of an unmarked brownstone on a picturesque, tree-and-gaslight-lined street, she transforms question marks into periods. It's therapy with a dash of magic.

The tarot reader's fee seems nominal for the sense of clarity I get from her sessions. She predicted the month I would hear the news of my novel's acceptance for publication. She told me the New Jersey apartment I was preparing to move into with Julian would leave me feeling like "Rapunzel in a tower," spelling the end of our marriage. She had no means of knowing that tower had been crumbling for quite some time. She told me my next relationship was cosmically doomed from the get-go, and that guy ended up setting my shoes on fire. She told me to avoid pages (as in, king, queen, knight, and page), who are "under eighteen emotionally." "You've got yourself a page" were words I came to dread.

Her insistence that clients record their sessions is further evidence of her accuracy. I have every session stored on my phone. You can always go back and listen. It's all on the record. With her track record of correct predictions, I believe what she tells me, though I simultaneously find this belief absurd. I traffic in facts, in what can be tangibly proven—with this one exception. I am both faithless and devout, holding these contradictory ideas simultaneously. That her business relies on referrals alone serves as justification from the part of me that believes to the part that doesn't—it's not as if she's sitting in some storefront, illuminated by a cheesy neon sign, inviting in any random passer-by. Dependence on referrals equals credibility. Would you recommend a doctor who misdiagnosed your condition?

Now I'm sending The Profiler, who does not believe in magic. She accepts my gift with an eye-roll.

"I don't understand why you waste an hour and a hundred dollars for her to tell you the same things I can see in five minutes," she says.

This time she is the one who could use advice. The Profiler is—drumroll—retiring. It's several years before she would have planned her voluntary exit from the Foreign Service. Her retirement comes about suddenly, while she's mid-assignment in Madrid, where she was supposed to be stationed for another two years. My ninety-year-old grandmother, a Brooklyn-born Seattle transplant who lives alone in the four-bedroom house once shared with a husband and her two daughters, has fallen ill and is unable to care for herself any longer.

Convinced my grandmother has months left to live, The Profiler agrees to take on her ultimate case. She's saved elderly tourists from a shipwreck in Greece, and yet somehow the care of her own mother is a greater challenge: it's personal. She can't leave it at the office at the end of the day. She knows she's doing the right thing, but moving from exciting Madrid into her mother's home in Seattle agitates her. She calls it "a regression to an unexciting past."

The daughter of a doctor and a housewife in Seattle, my mother had a privileged, upper-middle-class childhood. My grandmother volunteered at the hospital and recorded books on tape for the blind. She suffered from obsessive-compulsive disorder and depression, which she channeled into keeping a pristine home and making works of art that involved gluing thousands of single beads or beans onto canvases one at a time to create detailed pictures. One, of an Egyptian pharaoh, was hung in the display window of a department store downtown. My grandfather, a sharp and jovial ladies' man with a roving eye, taught my mother to work hard and follow the markets.

The Profiler excelled academically at her selective all-girls' school. Seeking escape from her stifling environment, she studied in Italy through the Experiment in International Living when she was sixteen, living with a host family and learning Italian. She fell in love with the energy and vibrancy, how people were out in the piazzas, not isolated in suburban houses on dark streets. She resolved to return to her dream country, and she did, for the PhD program she didn't finish because she met my father. After they were married, she became an Italian citizen herself—ironically settling down (at least for a time) not in Italy but in a house a mile from my grandparents' home. As my mother departed for her first Foreign Service post in the early 1980s, my grandmother, tired of my grandfather's affairs, divorced him.

My mother fled her "unexciting past" to live in Mexico, Italy, Greece, Venezuela, and Spain.

My grandfather married his girlfriend. Eventually they both passed away of old age. My grandmother lived on.

"I have more friends under the ground than walking on it," she would say.

THE PROFILER'S MOTHER drives her crazy much in the same way my mother feeds my own anxiety. Once, on a road trip, they got into an argument about whether some spot in the distance was a mountain or a cloud.

"She's so passive," my mother complains. "She could have done so much more with her life."

"Don't criticize."

I remind my mother that elder care is the most noble and important thing an adult child can do, that she is heroic for not putting my grandmother in a home, especially with American society's hegemonic view of old people as disposable.

Since Nathan and I broke up, I've been taking Baxter, whom I had trained as a therapy dog, to volunteer at a nursing home in Brooklyn. The staff are kind, but I see the sadness of those places. Residents hooked up to pouches of thick brown fluid. People who can't remember their names. Endless card games, puzzles, and cups of unnaturally colored gelatin snacks. Keeping my grandmother home is the kindest gesture my mother could make, even if she does resent leaving her powerful, stimulating diplomatic career.

"Why doesn't she want to do anything fun?" my mother complains of Grandma's OCD cleaning routines.

"She's ninety, she can do whatever she wants!"

I try to assure my mother that though she may have a plethora of mundane tasks to accomplish each day—shuttling to and from doctor's appointments, errands to the grocery store, the pharmacy, and that pancake house my grandmother likes—she's also never been more free: no more embassy responsibilities, long hours, work with Americans in trouble, or calls from Washington bureaucrats. Even if this new life consists of supervising my grandmother shuffling back and forth across the house, doing laundry, and running the dishwasher in a perpetual hamster wheel of cleanliness, my mother will, at the end of the day, be glad she did it. "You need to see the tarot reader," I tell her. "She'll give you clarity."

THE PROFILER FLIES in to Brooklyn on her way to Seattle and attends her tarot appointment. Though per the reader's policy my mother is technically not supposed to share her audio file with anyone, she sends me the recording of her session immediately afterward. I don't listen to it right away. I hold on to it in sweet anticipation. I will wait for my mother to settle into her new life so that when I listen I will already know whether the prophecies have come to fruition. Maybe, for a change, I'll be the one who gets to say I told you so.

I SETTLE IN front of my computer to listen to a heavyweight boxing championship between my two favorite fighters. The Profiler vs. the by-referral-only tarot reader.

THE PROFILER: I'm retiring, and it's not to a place I want to be.

THE BY-REFERRAL-ONLY TAROT READER: It's almost as if you're being sent into exile. I'm going to give you some homework. You've got three major cards . . . they're all [facing] down, and we need to get them up. It's like you've got a horse and buggy and you need to go some-where—but you put the horse in back of the buggy and push the horse.

TP: [*audible exhale*]

TBROTR: This shows the past. You spent a lot of time in this place grow-ing up not being able to wait to get out. You may have to create a journal for yourself on this exile. Like the journals that are written in prison.

TP: That makes sense.

TBROTR: The chariot card means finding ways to communicate with your environment. You need stimulation, and you need it all the time. You're not going to plaster yourself in a room and read books. Does this make sense?

TP: Yes it does.

TBROTR: Go out and explore. Unless you're on Antarctica, that's no problem. You're also afraid you might stay there, but you won't.

It's like a very extended vacation. You've got to study the culture and the people. Look at it like you got a vacation for a year. Some of the structure of your career involved doing things you didn't want to be involved in. Think about what you want. Do a list—purification to get to a higher state. Use this year to release the old life and put emphasis on what you want in your new life. You can really implement this time. You don't have to stay dormant! People in exile are mourning for their past. But you can be saying, *They gave me a big vacation. I'm moving into this new life.* And it is like a halfway house, between the old and the new.

The death card is a good card. It means death of people who were authorities above you. It's a release. It has to do with revolution. We're tying this all together: exile, revolution. You served your time. Like a soldier coming back and having to go to a retraining to move into his or her life again.

TP: That's true.

TBROTR: It's pulling you back to something you felt as a kid, and we need to yank you right out of that.

TP: I need to work on making those contacts and making it a positive transitional experience. Instead of just folding up.

TBROTR: Your fear is that you're off track, but the hermit is never off track. You're very intuitive about people. If nothing blocks you. It's like for me, if people come in and give me too much information, it's almost a detriment because it's like, you start figuring out where all that fits—that's why coming in and doing a reading straightforward is usually easier. As an intuitive kid you could read what was going on in your environment. Trust your internal guidance system. This is happening to bring you to a place where you'll know where you want to go. It's giving you time to think about it in a whole different way.

You're going through the locks to the ocean on the other side. This is about your family. You've worked it out, but feelings are always the last things to go.

Something adverse happens to place a person into growth. That's what this is about.

TP: Yes, that's what this is about.

TBROTR: It's like Tennessee Williams's play *The Rose Tattoo*—a girl is going off with a sailor, and he says, "Is this your first time?" And she says, "Every time is my first time." She's looking at it as a great new experience. Now, let's say if, the week before, she'd been beaten up by a sailor, she might look at the young sailor and go, *Oh my god, another sailor*. But she's not. This is a whole new sailor.

TP: This is very helpful.

TBROTR: What else are we looking at?

TP: Maybe, finding a new love in my life?

TBROTR: I'm going to use the same layout—a lot of this is relationship with your new life. You don't want to be with pages, that means people under eighteen emotionally. OH BOY. Lots of karma. The thing is, the atmosphere surrounding the question is interesting because it's "I'm just fine the way I am." Relationships can be a lot of work for you. You may have been involved with pages, so you've had to take care of them somehow. You're ready to break through all of this. You spent your whole life proving yourself. You don't need to prove yourself, with relationships or any other place. That's another family pattern that needs to be broken.

You put yourself on relationship hiatus for a while there. You've got four major cards here out of the ten. That's quite a bit in a ten-card layout. You're shifting from an old way of thinking to a new one.

There's no reason not to be in a relationship, but you don't want to be in one with someone who's not there for you. But break the pattern so those ones aren't attracted to you. You were the other side of the coin. You can read a person right away, you know pretty much who they are. Don't block that. Find out why you're getting that feeling.

When you're ready you'll find exactly who you want. You're not ready yet. You're making a sacrifice to get to a higher state. This is a huge card of metamorphosis, the hangman. You no longer have to run a kindergarten for relationships. It's time for the real thing.

In your new environment, spend some time with yourself, because she's the holder of all knowledge. The fact you're very intuitive will help you. It's like sending the specs out into the universe. Make a list of ten things you need and ten things you can't support. Like, being a loner isn't a bad thing, but if you're very social it's a problem. A lot of people only judge the positives, not looking at the other side of this fence.

TP: Yes, clarifying what I want clarifies me to others, so it will attract . . .

TBROTR: For a while you said "no vacancy." Now it would be saying, "I'm open to relationships." It may not happen in the next six months, but if you start doing the work and practice . . . you're going through a massive enough change as it is. You don't need to add to that. We'll see. You can have some fun with this. When you work on yourself, it changes the law of attraction. You wonder, *Why do I always get the same kind?* Well, it's the family stuff . . . it's the job she does. And you don't want to do that job anymore.

TP: That's very helpful. Thank you! Now, I'm concerned about my daughter's new boyfriend. I haven't met him, but from his Facebook photo and information, I don't think he's the right person for her, and I'm wondering if the relationship is going to last.

TBROTR: She's coming on Sunday . . .

TP: I don't know about the boyfriend. I know this is my transition, my thing to work on, but . . .

TBROTR: She might ask this on Sunday. Don't tell her we did this.

TP: No no, I won't.

TBROTR: She's got herself a page. That means a man under eighteen emotionally. But it will last a while because she's working something out with this. This looks like a bridge relationship. She was really unhappy about something else, and this sort of came along. It's working for her on a certain level right now, but I don't see this as necessarily lasting a long time because he's got some issues that he . . . and he's showing up as a page, but a good-natured page. It's almost like he's an anchor right now as opposed to someone to stay with permanently. Does that make sense?

TP: Yes.

TBROTR: She's more focused on her career right now. That's why the career queen is showing up right now. I've seen this before. This is fine now, a bridge, doesn't place too many demands on her. It will be interesting to see what she says. But this is what it is.

TP: That makes sense! . . . Is there something I should look towards in my thoughts of what I might want to develop as a career . . . next? Anything specific?

TBROTR: Am I headed to a solid avocation?

TP: Yeah, maybe. Or maybe there's not a solid thing there. It's not clear.

TBROTR: Let's see. This is you worrying about it. You're a worrier. You're moving into your own creativity, whatever it turns out to be.

Your imagination. Things coming to the surface from the subconscious. Don't think anything is frivolous. Communication may be involved. It may be something you can totally create yourself.

PERHAPS THE PROFILER and the by-referral-only tarot reader are not so different, but rather cut from the same cloth. Both make a living off their well-honed hunches from spending so much of their time close-reading people.

"So?" I ask when my mother comes back from her appointment. "Do you understand why I go to her now?"

"She has a really nice apartment in a great neighborhood. After Grandma, I should move near there. And I'll be closer to you."

AT MY APPOINTMENT on Sunday, I do ask about my career first, having no idea the reader has just told my mother the reason for my "bridge relationship" is that my career is my primary focus. The cards show I've been working on a certain project because it is the kind of thing that will please my mother: it isn't coming from my soul, but from the desire for external reward.

TBROTR: You did it as much for your mother as for yourself, and that proves something. It proves something to her as well. Now she can't say, "You should do that."

LM: I'm interested in a partnership of equals. I'm over the need or angst. Will there be someone? Anything I should avoid?

TBROTR: If you're going to swim the English Channel you have to work out in a pool for a while. You're in a holding position right now. The current relationship may just be a bridge. You've come to a new level where you say, *Where do I go from here?* You have to lift the mist and then you're there. They think you're gonna take care of them, and in the past you have. Now you like the ones that like whips and chains, so—no, I'm kidding. You're looking on all levels—emotionally, spiritu-ally, physically—for what you do need.

ANDY AND I finish crossing our bridge a few weeks after the reading. My mother needs a project, a next "avocation." She may have retired from the Foreign Service, but she'll always make use of her skills. Under her watchful care—new doctors, prescriptions, plans—my grandmother makes a full recovery. It's a miracle and a testament to The Profiler's abilities. However, now my mother is "stuck," as she phrases it, in a place she doesn't want to live.

"Why did I retire?" she asks on the phone. "Now she's better and I have nothing to do."

"She's better because of you. You're doing a great job!"

"I can't stand it here, though."

"Remember what the tarot reader said—you have to reframe. Use this time. This is a whole new sailor going through the locks to the ocean on the other side."

"I still don't understand why you don't just trust The Profiler."

"I trust the universe."

"No really. Why do you pay *her* to tell you such obvious things?"

"She references plays, she makes metaphors, there's imagery. It's fun."

This is a half-truth. What I can't admit is I rely on the reader for the same reason The Profiler, as a professional crisis handler, expertly saved those shipwreck survivors and yet was weighed down by the challenge of her own mother's care. It's personal. The tarot reader tells me what to expect without telling me what to do. I can avoid regressive meltdowns along the lines of, "Why won't you just let me live my life?" Consulting the reader—even if she is conning me a little—is gentler, if not on my bank account, then at least on my psyche, than the emotional charge that accompanies my mother's foretelling.

A note from the desk of

THE PROFILER

TAROT CARD READER: belief in fate?

As you know, I don't believe in fate or predestiny. Are innocent victims killed in terrorist attacks "fated" or "destined" to die? I can't see a reason in that or anything.

Liza had faith in her by-referral-only tarot card reader. But it was easy to agree with the clairvoyant's generalized comments: "You are moving to a new city. You need to meet new people, make new connections." Good suggestions, but obvious. Nothing she said was a revelation. Sometimes you may think, *Oh, if I hadn't gone to (fill in the blank), I wouldn't have (fill in the blank).* True, but you might have (fill in the blank) instead, somewhere else.

Liza apparently believes in fate but alleges she is skeptical. You can't prove one way or the other whether individual destiny exists. Certainly, it would be a lot of work for a god or "invisible force" to be determining the future for each of us. Personally, I don't believe prayer influences an outcome or the future. Calming people and helping them accept a sad situation—yes. But changing your tomorrow or bringing you what you pray for, no. If it happens, I believe it happens by chance.

Are things fated, or do changes or encounters in your life depend on your own actions, plus a dose of chance and coincidence? The Profiler opts for the latter. But decide for yourself. In the meantime, if you opt to spend money on a by-referral-only tarot card reader, you might feel calmer, but be skeptical of specific predictions.

SOMEBODY'S FRENCH GIRL

UN ESSAI EN QUATORZE MORCEAUX

UN

WE ALL SELF-MYTHOLOGIZE. It's why Didion's quote "We tell ourselves stories in order to live" is so famous. It explains my devotion to my by-referral-only tarot reader and Andy's obsession with the Legend of Dragon's Gate. The narrative overlay helps us find or create meaning where there is inherently none.

When it came to romantic relationships, though, I didn't realize how important "the story" was until, the summer before Andy and I committed to each other, I'd signed up for JDate out of sheer curiosity. As a serial monogamist I'd never before had space to try it. Through JDate I met a jazz musician. Handsome. Curly brown hair. Texas accent. How adorable is a Texan Jewish boy, tough and gentle at the same time, rugged yet scholarly? He constantly traveled the world on tour with his trio. He would have invited me along. I would have had my writing sojourns in cafés and hotels in Sydney, Tokyo, Paris, wherever his jazz travels took him—pretty much my dream of the rooted-yet-unconventional life. He was fun and smart and open about looking for the right woman, his future wife.

We had a handful of lively dates on which we talked late into the night at bars and restaurants all over Brooklyn. Yet after each one, I felt a nagging sense of not looking forward to seeing him again. I tried to pinpoint why.

Was something off? I tried to assess what it was about him, or about me, but it wasn't either of us. It was the system. Our rendezvous felt like rounds of a job interview. When he kissed me at the end of the first date, it felt as if I was performing in an "end-of-first-date" scene in a twee romantic comedy. I was a sucker for the story. I wasn't into the thought of "It all started when Mommy swiped to the right" as what I'd one day tell my kids about The Beautiful And Romantic Origins Of Their Parental Units.

Online dating has hatched beautiful marriages for many and introduced people whose paths might never have crossed otherwise. Discrediting it made dating more challenging because going online made looking easy. You could distill so much about somebody from a profile, as my mother would say, but finding a man on JDate felt like shopping, a simplification of an organic process that was, like a good story, reliant on synchronicity, serendipity, luck, chance, and circumstance. Of course, if I'd met the right person online, I'd be singing a different tune. "How we met" would simply become *part* of the story. We'd have many others to tell after "and then he (or I) swiped to the right." I was still resisting my mother's tactics: dating sites and apps turn us all into little profilers, making fast assessments based on surface criteria. If Jewish Jazz Musician had been the right person, it wouldn't have mattered if we'd met online or if he'd dropped like a rock from the sky and landed on my living room floor. But at the time I saw it as not working out because we'd met in this intentional way.

The kicker with Jewish Jazz Musician, though, was when I introduced him to a friend on my stoop when he came to pick me up for brunch and a walk. My friend, genuinely curious, asked how we met. "Online," I answered. I didn't think anything of it. But after brunch, as JJM and I walked, he brought up "the thing you said to your friend." I'd forgotten all about it. Turned out he'd been stewing about my openness, about our "how we met" story.

"Don't tell people that. We have to come up with a better 'how we met' story."

"You're right, there needs to be a better story."

Except I wasn't going to lie to my friends, so this better story would not be with him. Feeling as if our story—or any story—was something to hide was a red flag. Maybe I was starting to profile after all.

DEUX

Here it is. The "how we met" story. I love it so much, I wish I could say I invented it.

My friend New Age Kassi and I are attending a big literary conference in Chicago. I've loved New Age Kassi since the first day we turned up in the same class in grad school, since I first heard her joke that "you could serve bread" on her earrings. It was true. She's from Kentucky and has lost all but a slight touch of twang. Blond with a black streak in her hair, beautiful, spiritual, and with a striking intelligence, New Age Kassi is the most stylish and wittiest in every room she walks into while also being your spiritual counselor and Buddhist-Episcopalian priestess. The epitome of the wise-friend type, the first person you think of when you need advice. Getting to spend three days straight with her is one of the reasons I'm excited about being at the conference.

Early the first morning, we're in queue at the hotel lobby Starbucks. I scan the pastry case for my usual egg-and-cheese concoction. They are sold out. Only muffins and pastries line the windowed shelf. Sugary breakfast items make me queasy. Can't do sweetness on an empty stomach. I spot a single cheese Danish and opt for that as a compromise, because even though it's sugary, it has the word "cheese." I order my latte and the Danish, pay the cashier, and wait. The cashier has not yet reached into the case for it when I hear a male voice at the adjacent register: "And that Danish to go." His more go-getting cashier opens the pastry case, angling at my Danish with her tongs.

"Excuse me, I already paid for that," I tell my cashier. She apologizes and quickly crosses tongs with her colleague, capturing the Danish and dropping it into a small paper baglet she hands me. It happens in an instant, all before I can glimpse the rival orderer-of-Danish. Meaning, he could be anyone—a grandpa, a bike messenger, a fat tourist, a skinny tourist. As I turn, I blurt, "But you can have half." I don't know who said it. I mean, it was me, but it wasn't a forethought. The words just jumped out of my mouth.

Then I'm facing him, and the whole world around me has stopped. That moment in a movie when everything darkens and freezes and there's a spotlight on us—in that instant, he and I are alone in that hotel lobby Starbucks.

He is not a grandpa, a bike messenger, a fat tourist, or a skinny tourist. He is, by my standards at least, an arrestingly attractive man. Academically scruffy. Wearing a conference lanyard. Brown eyes glowing with intelligence and intensity behind the frames of his very literary glasses. Here, in all his glory, stands Half-Danish.

We introduce ourselves. He's just finished presenting on a panel. He's an author. A semi-famous one. When I Google him later, I will discover his many stellar reviews and awards. I cut the Danish in half on the milk-and-sugar station and hand it over to him.

"If this situation happened in reverse I wouldn't have done the same for you," he says. "I guess I'm not that nice."

"Well now next time maybe you will be," I say, smiling.

When he invites New Age Kassi and me to his reading that evening, there's no question that I'm going. I already love our story: "He tried to steal my Danish, well not exactly steal, he tried to buy it out from under me after I'd already paid for it. Before I even saw him, I offered him half. We've been sharing ever since." Awww. Gross. But cute. At least admit it's a good "how we met" story. Perhaps, like the Danish, sickeningly sweet, especially first thing in the morning, but still.

TROIS

Here is what my mother meant when she said I should wait for some "truly special guy." So the truly special guy lived in Chicago. Geographical distance was no matter when it came to love. New Age Kassi sipped her soy latte and agreed to accompany me to his reading that evening.

QUATRE

At the reading, Half-Danish killed it, to the applause of his packed room-ful of fans. I can't remember when he and I exchanged phone numbers, only that he texted me later: "Lost track of you somewhere. If you're still in the neighborhood, a bunch of us are drinking at Rainbo, at Damen and Division. Hope to see you."

In order to lose track of me, he had to be keeping track of me . . . and he hoped to see me . . . the signs of his interest were so clear, they weren't even signs. They were statements, plain as a Starbucks croissant.

CINQ

At the bar, I found out Half-Danish was also a backgammon aficionado. He said he was good. I challenged him. I could count my areas of self-confidence on one hand, and my skill as a backgammon player was up there. A friend taught me to play during a college semester abroad in the Netherlands, and I soon became a backgammon hustler, adoring the combination of strategy and luck it took to win. I played on European trains and in the coffee shops of Amsterdam. I offended a rug salesman in Istanbul's Grand Bazaar by winning game after game. I taught my ex, Nathan. Backgammon became a habit as addictive as his smoking. We played tournaments as we ate Giant Salads. "I'm pretty sure I can beat you," I told Half-Danish. He promised to bring a backgammon board to the conference the next afternoon, and we would reconvene to play. I got a feeling I'd finally met my match.

An award-winning, semi-famous author with a great career, a pro-fessor and intellectual who was also fun to hang out and have drinks and conversation with—even The Profiler couldn't disapprove. I was also intimidated: he was too smart, too award winning, too cool for me. He was at the conference not as a mere attendee, but as a Featured Person. There to get paid rather than paying to be there. I felt small and young and dizzy all at once in his presence. He was nothing like my man-child, whiskey-hoovering, never-had-a-savings-account, and/or searching-for-the-meaning-of-life-while-reliving-lost-youth, and/or emotionally abusive banker exes. Here was an artist and a professional who was financially stable yet more than just good on paper. He was unconventionally handsome with a sexy, earthy vibe about him. Him, I could definitely imagine kissing. I finally understood what The Profiler had been talking about. So I'd have to move to freezing Chicago, but at least it was a big, cosmopolitan city that surely had a capoeira group. For Half-Danish it would be worth it. The pastry order that changed my life. It felt like waking up.

SIX

The next day at the conference, I paid little attention to the speakers, the vast hall of books and networking opportunities. Anything I'd originally come there for, I ignored, my thoughts trained on Half-Danish. I kept glancing at my phone even knowing there was no missed call or text message because I'd turned the volume all the way up so as not to miss one. The lights and conversations and patterned convention center carpeting all blended together, a whirl of noise and literary types and scholars and grad students frantically hobnobbing in the aisles and little pop-up bars off to the side where exhausted conference-goers paused for coffee, Red Bull, and wine. As if in my own little personal scene out of *Fear of Flying*, I was already inhabiting a fantasy world in my mind in which, though I'd only just met him, I ran away here, to Chicago, to Half-Danish: We'd write together in hip Wicker Park cafés. Read early drafts of each other's work and have deep, impactful conversations about it. Travel the world. Occasionally go to synagogue.

In the afternoon, I went to his book signing and stood in line with his other fans to buy and have him inscribe my copy of his new book. "For Liza, from whom I will soon extract many points," he wrote. Soon? He already had. But I knew he was talking about backgammon. A couple hours later (he was reliable!), my phone lit up with Half-Danish's name. I waited exactly two rings (no desperation!), caught my breath, and answered with what I hoped was a cool enough hello. My organs turned to jelly at the sound of his slightly raspy voice. "I'm really sorry," he said. "I'm not going to be able to meet this afternoon. Rain check for tomorrow?"

"He cancelled on our backgammon date," I told New Age Kassi when we met back up for lunch in the conference center. "It's all over before it ever even began."

"He probably had something he needed to do," she said, my beacon of reason that dark afternoon of Half-Danish's absence.

Sure enough, twenty-four hours later he was standing outside the hotel toting a backgammon board, looking even better than the day before. He smoked a cigarette on the sidewalk. His smile melted my bones. I'd chosen my outfit carefully that morning—faux-leather leggings, high-heeled wingtip Doc Martens (yes they exist), a white T-shirt, and New Age Kassi's soft black cardigan. I'd thought Half-Danish would ferry me to one of those hip cafés in Wicker Park, but there wasn't time. We headed for the hotel Starbucks where we'd met, but finding it closed, ended up in the hotel basement. (This was getting less and less romantic by the minute.) At least there was a carpeted lounge area. We set up the board, talking about our lives and histories as we played. I tried to be witty while playing well and failed at doing either. "This is so embarrassing, this never happens," I said. Half-Danish emerged victorious from round after round. I wasn't even remotely a challenging opponent. I felt humiliated, having talked about how unbeatable I was. My face flushed. I tried blaming my losses on terrible dice rolls.

Because the game is a mixture of strategy and luck, if the dice don't work in your favor in backgammon, no matter how sharp your strategy, you're going to lose.

Unless you're a really, truly exceptional player, as I was rapidly learning that Half-Danish, in addition to being handsome and a genius and a semi-famous author, was. It aggravated me and made my admiration for him grow tenfold. I took my losses to heart, demanding rematches only to be beaten again. I took the tournament way more seriously than he did. As he gained victory after victory, I tried to impress him with my go-to Mexico City stories. These seemed to work better than my capoeira stories, which just made him look at me as if I'd told him I was part of a circus or a cult. I worried maybe he thought I was really an athlete, and that an athlete and a chain-smoker wouldn't go together. Then the subject turned to relationships.

Half-Danish said he was recently out of a six-year one with a live-in girlfriend. They'd still been together when he went to Paris for his French book launch, and while he was there he'd had a "really intense thing" with a French girl. So much so that when he came back, he broke up with his girlfriend. He'd only just met The French Girl, but that was all it took for him to go home and end things with the woman he'd thought he would be with for life. Whose name was all over the acknowledgments section of his books.

Sudden things happen that free us from situations that are no longer serving us: The Helicopter Pilot swooping in, pushing Nathan to the point of committing The Destruction, and then flying off again, into the ether, or New Jersey. If it hadn't been for The French Girl, whoever she was, Half-Danish would not be single at this moment. He would be living with his longtime partner and not sitting here, at the backgammon board with me. The French Girl had granted him *liberté*.

I told him about my separation at twenty-seven from my high school–sweetheart-turned-banker ex and our subsequent divorce.

"Do you think you'd get married again?" Half-Danish asked.

"Yes," I said, maybe too enthusiastically, so I added, "if I met the right person. How about you?"

"I don't believe in marriage," he said.

Oh.

"Why not?"

"Marriage tends to lead to babies."

Doesn't want kids. Okay . . . I didn't necessarily need to have kids. I backtracked.

"I don't want marriage as a gateway to all that," I said. "It's about partnership."

After a few more rolls of the dice and another humiliating loss, he leaned over the backgammon board and kissed me. I may have lost the backgammon tournament, but really, I won! Flash-forward to our life together in Chicago: house on some tree-lined street, writing, teaching, happy hour at Rainbo, trips to his family's place in the suburbs for Shabbat.

"Do you still have your room?" he asked between kisses.

My reality was again rapidly turning into a scene out of *Fear of Flying*.

"I checked out before we met up," I said. "Next time." I smiled, hoping there would be a next time.

Oddly, he got up and started looking around for a private place in the basement. There wasn't one, and I had to leave anyway. I was late to meet New Age Kassi in the lobby to catch our flight back to New York.

He walked me outside, where we kissed again. A light rain began to fall. He told me he was coming to New York in a month, to give a reading, and would I be there? Why yes indeed, yes I would, I said.

"I'll see you then," he said, and it took all my effort not to flip down the sidewalk out of the sheer joy of this promise. I turned my back and walked away without turning around. I feared I would run back and kiss him like at the end of some cheesy romantic comedy. I had a month. In that month, I would get my life together. I would clean my apartment. He could come over. He would see that my apartment was so clean and my life so together. He would see that I was worthy of him. We would officially date and trade weekends between Brooklyn and Chicago. Yes, yes, this was how it was going to play out, because we'd had a beautiful start to our story, and what does a good start make you do but continue on to see where it will go?

SEPT

"You ready? Our flight leaves in an hour!" New Age Kassi said.

In the taxi to the airport, I told her of my hopes for Half-Danish and myself, how in a month, my entire life was going to change.

"It's happening so fast!" she said, with a smile. "Should you ask your mom to profile him?"

HUIT

Despite its correctness, I was still resistant to my mother's profiling and didn't want to encourage her already rampant "suggesting," her unsolicited advice about everything. Yet the time had come to get over my pride and stubbornness and listen to her already. She had been right too many times to ignore. The ideal opportunity presented itself. Before coming to New York, Half-Danish was making a stop in Seattle to give a reading.

I would send my mother to profile him. She would be so happy. I would be sure I wasn't making another mistake. This time, I would listen. But I was confident she would approve.

Regardless, it was a big step. Where I once chafed at her meddling, I'd now seek out her counsel. It wasn't only the perfect opportunity for me. It was for her, too: *My mother needs an outlet, and I need to make better choices.* For once, we were perfectly matched.

NEUF

I called her the night I got home from Chicago. I was walking Baxter around Prospect Heights, fantasizing about doing the same down the streets of the Windy City. I longed so much to give up my winter coat, but I'd need an even heavier one there. For Half-Danish, it would be worth it.

"Mom, you were right," I said. "You're going to have to profile anyone I'm thinking about getting serious with from now on."

I told her all about Half-Danish, my realization about what was really out there, romantically—not only did he not have to be a project, he could be brilliant, kind, handsome, smart, lauded . . . He could be Half-Danish. "He's coming to New York in a month, but I can hardly wait that long. He'll be in Seattle first, for his new book tour. Will you go? I mean, don't tell him you're you, just be a reader who's there—and profile him. I'll only see him again if you approve."

It was my mother's turn to be delighted. And surprised.

"Sure, I'll go," she said, happy to be on assignment again. At last, I had come to my senses enough to take advantage of hers.

DIX

My mother called me as soon as she walked in the door of my grandmother's house after Half-Danish's reading in Seattle.

"Well?" I wanted to jump right in. "Let me have it."

"Better than the other ones," she said.

"Yes!"

"There were a few things . . . he wore a ratty sweatshirt."

"A dark-blue hoodie?"

"Yes."

"I think he always wears that. Either he has ten of those hanging in his closet or he's always doing laundry."

"It was schleppy looking. But that's the thing now I guess. His story . . . something about a lesbian dwarf? Too weird for me."

"But overall?"

"He was comfortable with the audience, at ease. He could relate to people well. He's Jewish and smart, and he'd be good for you because he's not good for someone taller."

I laughed.

"Okay, verdict?"

"Approved."

ONZE

The elusive approval! At last! The days of March passed at the pace of hair pulled out strand by strand. I spent the entire month reading his book, anticipating seeing him, and telling every poor girlfriend who would listen the story of how I met my Half-Danish in Chicago. I was bothered that he hadn't called or texted, but was comforted by spotting his picture in the *New York Times Book Review*. He sat on a balcony, staring into the lens as if about to reveal an essential life secret only he knew. He was wearing "the sweatshirt." The reviewer wrote:

Beware, [Half-Danish] seems to say, the false hope of perfect solutions. Because love itself is never a panacea. On the contrary, it generally rips up your life rather than sewing it back together. Still, even knowing it will hurt, we always seem to come back for more.

Yes. When a friend asked if I didn't think it strange I hadn't heard from him since the backgammon encounter, I patiently explained that Half-Danish was on a *national book tour*. He was kind of busy getting his picture in the *New York Times*.

One friend lent me a bunch of outfits to choose from for his reading. A few volunteered to attend the reading for moral support and to see the mystical pastry man in the flesh.

Finally, early April and the evening of his reading rolled around. I met my friends at a bar beforehand and nervously drank a glass of water. We walked down the street to the venue. Half-Danish was standing outside, smoking a cigarette. My heart fluttered like a hummingbird had taken up residence inside my chest, and I started to sweat. I tried to play it cool.

"Hey!" he greeted me. "You came."

"Wouldn't miss it." *Wouldn't miss it?* Ugh. How desperate.

He made some distracted small talk and was called inside. He was probably nervous before his event. We'd talk more afterward, when he was relaxed. Nerves, yes. Certainly that's what it was. His reading was brilliant (The Profiler was right that his stories were "weird," but genius-weird, Saunders-weird. It wasn't her taste so she just didn't get it). He had the audience engaged and laughing during his Q&A afterward. He circulated around talking to his friends and fans. He wasn't looking for me. Disappointed, I was about to call it quits. I'd imagined the whole thing. It was just a conference hookup. I was another warm body for his reading. I went to say congratulations and goodbye before going home to drink half a bottle of wine.

"Hey," he said. "Do you want to go grab a drink with us?"

Do birds want to fly? Does the earth want to turn? Do stars want to shine?

"Um, sure, I guess. Where?"

We reconvened at a bar around the corner from the venue, but he sat in a corner eating pizza with his sister the whole time. I played pool, drank some sauvignon blanc, and asked my friends if it seemed as if he was ignoring me. They concurred. He was. I didn't understand why he'd invited me to the reading or this gathering. Disappointed, I went outside to volta ao mundo. To my surprise he appeared behind me. We talked about apartment ownership in Chicago vs. New York, some mystery meeting he had early the following morning, and other superficial topics, until a silence entered between us, and he broke it with, "So . . . we made out a bunch in Chicago."

Finally, getting somewhere, I thought.

"Yeah, and?"

Right then his friend burst out the door.

"The waitress has a question about the check."

Leaving the question hanging, Half-Danish went back inside. The mystery continued. Was he going to say, "That should never have happened?" Or, "We should do it again?" I was left with more questions. When he came back out, he was with his friends and his sister. He said goodbye and left. I had spent the previous month thinking about him. Reading his work every day. Sending my mother to his reading. I'd even gotten her first positive profile. I thought we'd gotten it right this time. But he hadn't been thinking of me at all. I'd imagined the whole thing.

DOUZE

My enlightenment as to what really happened came from a source I wouldn't have anticipated: *Playboy* magazine. Half-Danish had mentioned writing an essay on the underground casinos of Paris. I flipped through the magazine at a West Village newsstand, so hungry for answers I didn't even care who saw me reading *Playboy*. In New York City nobody gave a second look. I should start by saying the article was amazing. Well written. A fantastic story. I'd read anything this guy wrote. A true talent.

As for the rest, I could say, *What an asshole!* Or *He was totally dishonest!* Or whatever bitter blaming thing. But I'm not interested in that. This was fascinating stuff, the contents of this article. The behind-the-scenes scenario was that Half-Danish had been obsessed with The French Girl the entire time. It wasn't what I'd thought it had been, a fleeting thing that showed him he was in the wrong relationship and it was time to let go. Since he met her, he couldn't stop thinking about how to see her again, so much so that he pitched an article to *Playboy* about the underground casinos of Paris. (Turns out there really weren't any, at least not in the way they'd been described to him.) The article gets meta about his pitching the article just to get back to this girl. It's really very clever. The Profiler was right: he was a brilliant mind with a touch of strangeness. The French Girl turns out to be the essay's primary subject, his longing for her and the brief time they spent together. And then, there it was, online: he tells his interviewer, a porn star, what he hadn't told me:

> *I've been waiting for a Parisian to come visit me for nearly two months now, and she'll be here tomorrow, which is amazing, but that level of amazing after all that anticipation is the kind of thing that gets me feeling joyous and thus hypersocial, and that can lead to silliness, so I figure it's better I do what I can to monk out like a dorky writer guy in advance of her arrival and just kinda . . . long.*

He'd been biding his time while awaiting her arrival, and I was part of the "silliness" contained in a brief, fleeting moment within his own waiting period. I was less than a bit player in his story, a background actor, whereas he had been my leading man, my main event, capturing the role without even having to audition. I'd thought I had the beginnings of a great story with him, while he had a better one all along, with her. He wrote about it, got national magazines to publish it, spoke openly about it in interviews. I was a distraction from his attempt at being "good"—and she was the one flying back to Chicago. At least the advantage of his being semi-famous was that I could find my answer in a magazine and on the internet. A ghosting mystery is worse than knowing an answer, even if it's not one you wanted to hear.

"He's seeing someone else," I told my mother.

"Then he wasn't the one," she said. "That's all right. We'll find somebody better."

"But there's a flaw in your plan, Mom. The French Girl X factor. You can tell if someone's worth pursuing, but that doesn't guarantee he'll be interested."

"Well, not everyone's going to want to be with you or me. Maybe the timing's wrong or they have somebody else. He shouldn't have kissed you, but he felt attracted to you in that moment. He didn't encourage you afterward because he already had The French Girl. Why don't you go back on JDate?"

"I'll do it if you do," I said.

But even then I knew I wouldn't, because my mother wouldn't online-date either. The system she trusted was her own.

Because I used to indulge in the self-defeating pleasures of online lurking, what I did use my internet time for was attempting to find out more about The French Girl. I needed to understand. Some stalking—specifically, looking through Half-Danish's friend list for women who lived in Paris and homing in on the gorgeous stunner who *must* have been her—revealed she'd RSVP'd to a Facebook event for a gallery opening in Bushwick in two weeks. The French Girl was going to be in New York! I dragged a friend to the opening under the guise of doing "research for a novel" I was writing about Facebook stalking. We drank bad gallery wine and looked at ugly sculptures and talked to partygoers all night, but I didn't see any French girl. Months later, I glimpsed a rare post on Half-Danish's page with The French Girl in it. She wasn't the French girl I'd picked out. I'd had the wrong French girl. I'd even failed at trying to increase my own misery.

TREIZE

Half-Danish and I never corresponded again. We'd connected on Facebook the morning of that fated meeting at the lobby Starbucks, and Facebook later informed me he married The French Girl. She moved to Chicago for him. It led me to understand Sudden Marriage Syndrome: When you are so beloved you even change the mind of somebody who waffles about marriage. When somebody simply loves you so much that skepticism and doubt fall away, and there is only one option.

Two years later, I would read a brilliant feminist text that a brilliant feminist author friend recommended about the Wives of Modernism— Zelda Fitzgerald, Vivienne Eliot, and Jane Bowles, among other writers whose *husbands'* names grace required-reading lists. To my shock and nefarious delight, in an autobiographical interlude on page 226, the author begins calling out none other than Half-Danish: "Do you know that massive novel displayed everywhere lately . . . the one that could serve as a blunt murder weapon? The author is a guy I once knew in Chicago, was friends with for a while." Transfixed, I read on. "We had a falling out after a brief and stupid hook-up." *Whoa.* "After that, I always kind of hated him." *I feel ya, sister.* "He tells me his work will be the longest first-person novel EVER . . . He is pulling out his cock and comparing it with those writers with whom he will be compared." *Sounds like maybe I dodged another bullet with this guy.* I hoped The French Girl was having a better story than this—surely, as The One He Was Waiting For, she must have been. The Brilliant Feminist Author continues: "He writes, I imagine, in the tradition of neurotic men who treat women as objects but are forgiven for their insight and sensitivity, in the tradition of falling in love and into beautiful girls." *Beautifully articulated. And she is way harsher than The Profiler.*

I too had been a "brief and stupid hook-up," and barely. Now the person I really wanted to meet was The Brilliant Feminist Author. I wanted her and New Age Kassi and *every* brilliant feminist author to gather for a regular literary salon and have a riveting conversation that would kill it on the Bechdel Test. The French Girl—herself a novelist—could join in. Create a tribe of feminist authors so brilliant our movement would be named, and they'd write a book about the husbands one day.[8]

QUATORZE

The dice hadn't rolled in my favor, but that fateful pastry order did change my life: Half-Danish gave me something more precious than a glittery "how we met" story. Appropriately from one writer to another, he'd unknowingly gifted me the precise language with which to articulate what exactly it was that I wanted: A love in which we were willing to go to the ends of the earth for each other. To make huge changes for each other. To be the person for whom the answer to the big questions was always yes. A person with whom I'd never feel complacent, and vice versa. There was no Half-Danish-shaped hole in my heart, because now I knew. I wanted to be somebody's French Girl.

Sometimes, we stay in the wrong relationship for years before someone comes along who shows us we should have moved on long ago. In Half-Danish's case, The French Girl was that: Goodbye six-year relationship. Goodbye Paris. Married after he thought he did not believe in marriage. She was his French Girl, and he was her Whole Danish. It's a beautiful story. It just wasn't mine.

---

8 With an appearance by Half-Danish in a footnote.

A note from the desk of

THE PROFILER

"IF THIS SITUATION happened in reverse I wouldn't have done the same for you," he says.

A verbal clue, Liza. You missed it. Right there, at the Starbucks counter when you first met him. Half-Danish told you what you refused to pick up on, but later found out. The Profiler only knew what you gushingly told her on the phone—and based on that, Half-Danish sounded great. A recognized, published writer with awards. A university professor. A guest speaker at a national writers conference. Intelligent, single, and Jewish. Nothing wrong with that résumé and, obviously, an attraction between them. So, The Profiler stamped an initial approval.

Not aware of any negatives, I joined the audience at Half-Danish's book tour in Seattle. Another guy in a well-worn hoodie. But with self-confidence, humor, and poise, he entertained the public, reading from his latest work. Eloquent, good stage presence. But weird stories. *This guy has a strange mind*, I thought. But, being in my sixties, I conceded that his literary audience was probably a much younger, hipper group. I reported back my approval, with a few qualifiers: sloppy outfit and strange tales. Positives outweighed negatives.

Liza lost game after game of backgammon. He sealed his victory with a kiss. The conqueror wins. Was he just playing with Liza? Maybe he was attracted, but also dishonest.

Then came other signs that Liza didn't want to see. Time passing. Silence. If someone is interested in you, he/she is proactive—calls, emails, texts . . . communication. The kiss was a tantalizing empty promise. Don't be fooled. What is he telling you by his actions—or inaction? Liza waited and hoped. Was he reaching out toward her? No. Read the signs. If some-one is interested in you, they will show it. And maybe that line about not being interested in marriage was just a way to discourage Liza. Half-Danish was obviously interested in marriage with The French Girl. Moral of the story: Even if an unexpected encounter gets your heart fluttering, listen to verbal cues. Discover what he is telling you, even if it's not what you want to hear.

ICKY SWEATER

WHAT THE PROFILER does with her spare time during retirement is, true to form, collect her pension and take trips. Antarctica to see the penguins and take a polar plunge (yes, that's a dip in the thirty-four-degree Antarctic waters in nothing but a swimsuit). Hot air ballooning over Bagan, Myanmar. Snorkeling in Palau, Raja Ampat, and Fiji. Yellowknife to celebrate New Year's Eve on a frozen lake watching the Aurora Borealis, drinking champagne slushies. A Viking fest in York, England. She'll go to the farthest ends of the earth to escape her own mother, whom, aligned in a familiar pattern, she finds difficult to live with. Elder care isn't easy under any circumstances, but my grandmother won't leave the house because the napkins need ironing. Her vision too poor to make OCD bead art anymore, she channels that energy fully into obsessive-*cleaning* disorder. She spends her days washing things and running machines that wash things. My mother, who can't stay still or spend one single day inside the house, lives for her own escapes. When she is home, she analyzes and reports on my grandmother's moves with her spy-trained focus.

"She has a Miralax obsession," my mother says. "She doesn't understand bowel movements aren't exactly regular each day at the same time. She's angry at getting old, even when I do nice things for her—take her out to dinner, for walks in the park, to the movies . . ."

"She's ancient, Mom. Let her do what she wants."

"But she's difficult. She complains. You know what else she does? She takes her hearing aid out, asks a question, then says, 'I can't hear you' when I reply. I have to speak slowly and say things over and over."

"You do that anyway."

"She doesn't appreciate what I do. She's lucky she can still walk."

When The Profiler is in Seattle, she can often be found jailbreaking to Vancouver and Oregon. Any getaway, no matter how close or how brief, is preferable to arguing over how she caught my grandmother using the step stool to water a plant when that is forbidden lest she fall. My grandmother counters that my mother is a dictator with no sense of humor.

When my mother travels, she gets home-care aides to check in on my grandmother so she can check out and then check herself into a five-star hotel (Profiler interjection: "or cute B&B")

During one of her trips to Portland, my mother texts me a snapshot of a sweater. A second text follows.

MOM: Do you want this sweater?

THAT sweater? Baffling. I scrutinize the photograph. Beneath its brown fake-fur collar, the sweater is divided into five thick horizontal chunks that match and yet look like pieces of different sweaters forced to cohabitate. The top is navy blue with what appear to be Greek symbols or a row of musical half notes. The next section down is heather gray with blue triangles. Then comes a brown section with a vaguely Native American design. Beneath that, another thick gray stripe lined with little blue triangles. The bottom third of the sweater is navy blue with the same Greek musical note pattern as the one circling the shoulders.

Suffice it to say it's a hideous sweater.

I'd think she is kidding, but my mother's not the type to joke. Does she, seeing years of my personal style of black clothes, colors-not-found-in-nature hair, and chunky platform boots, really think this hiking-in-a-snowy-wood sweater says "me"? If she is attracted to this sweater, how can I trust her to screen men? With our clearly differing tastes in something as basic as which body coverings we find aesthetically pleasing, how can I count on her to apply the right set of criteria for me instead of subconsciously choosing a younger version of a man she'd pick for herself, for her own needs and tastes? It doesn't bode well for her wanting me to trust the vetting process she'll do on my behalf when I send her a new interest to profile.

Like a majority of moms, The Profiler means well. She wants more than anything for her only child to be successful and loved. I love her and her good intentions, among other things, but I will be doing none of the above in that sweater.

I text back.

ME: I guess I could wear it to an ugly sweater party.
MOM: Oh, okay. No icky sweater.

She respects my wishes, and I do not receive the sweater. But this is not the last of what becomes known as Icky Sweater. Icky Sweater comes to permeate our lives.

Mother-daughter communication can be challenging. Mothers have ideas for daughters' choices with which daughters do not necessarily agree. The Profiler dispenses freely with unsolicited advice conforming to said ideas. Number one of course is what I should seek in a partner, from employment to appearance and defining characteristics. Then, in no particular order of importance: "Learn the stock market." "Don't bother with little articles. Write books. Sell screenplays. GO FOR THE BIG SUCCESS!"

Our conversation consists of an ongoing stream of well-intentioned, unsolicited advice from her and my lame attempts to rechannel the discussion into the realm of ideas and feelings. Icky Sweater has become a humorous way we can communicate our frustrations with each other, especially as our communication has migrated into texting. Texting was not invented for people like my mother. The photograph of the sweater has become a shorthand conversation-ender. Nothing says "no more" like the sweater.

MOM: Lize, have you put your savings into that IRA I set up for you? Gone to any of those financial seminars at Charles Schwab yet? You really need to start showing an interest in investing.
ME: ICKY SWEATER

Or:

ME: Have you been showing an interest in meeting new people in Seattle?

MOM: ICKY SWEATER

And another time:

MOM: I hope you're still not spending money on those tarot readings.

ME: ICKY SWEATER

And:

MOM: Met anyone interesting yet? Still think JDate is worth another try.

ME: ICKY SWEATER

ME: How is Grandma today?

MOM: ICKY SWEATER

And my all-time favorite, career-related:

MOM: What does your agent say about your book? Has she gotten back to you yet? Are there a lot of corrections to make? You should let me read it and I can give you suggestions for improvements.

ME: SWEATER SWEATER SWEATER

Just like that, we have a much-needed shorthand, a code to communicate frustration in a way that diffuses the situation and makes it funny instead. Icky Sweater was our own personal emoticon before emoticons became ubiquitous, a way to inform yet not offend, to diffuse those inevitable flare-ups of our incompatibilities. Who'd have thought an ugly sweater could be the thing that helps communication and relieves strain? Sometimes a photograph really can step in where words fail. Mothers and daughters who aren't always in sync (i.e., every mother and daughter . . . unless you're one of those magical-unicorn, conflict-free, best-friend duos) should have a means to end what would otherwise become heated discussions in a way that makes them smile and not fight. "No hard feelings, but that's it on that topic," my mother says. Feel free to raid our sweater drawer—or maybe you'll find your own special symbol.

THE PROFILER AND I have been sending Icky Sweater back and forth for years. Our relationship has improved because of it. It finally occurs to me to ask her why she thought I might like it in the first place.

"I thought the sweater looked nice," she says. "Earth tones, warm, kind of Northwest Indian motif . . . I really thought you might like it. Colors are good, natural tones. Authentic looking. Warm wool. Fun collar. Authentic, not-glitzy, practical, attractive sweater. You were in NYC, which is cold, and I thought this looked fun and Northwesty. Looking at it now, it still looks good to wear with jeans or black pants. Plus it's good wool. So Icky Sweater is still nice. It would look good on you!"

Staring at the photograph of the sweater, I wonder if maybe it isn't actually as hideous as I'd initially thought. Maybe if she'd gotten it for me I would have worn it. But probably not.

LOVE AND DEATH AND FAITH AND FATE AND MARINE IGUANAS

Well, here we are, Mr. Pilgrim, trapped in the amber of this moment.
There is no why.

—**Kurt Vonnegut, *Slaughterhouse-Five***

I MAKE APPOINTMENTS WITH my by-referral-only tarot reader the way most people go to the dentist.

In the spring of 2012, I land a summer job in Beijing teaching essay writing to Chinese students hoping to attend U.S. colleges. It's the farthest I'll have traveled alone, hired by people I've never met, about to be paid more than I have the right to earn in such a short period of time. As with most things that seem too good to be true, it is.

The by-referral-only tarot reader senses this, too, as she looks down at the cards and tells me not to go. My soul mate will be revealed on my summer travels, and going to China would throw things off. His name begins with a *J*.

". . . He's a traveler, you'd like a traveler. He'll be photographing . . . sea turtles. I don't know why I'm picking up a camera with this guy. It seems like he's very literate, which is another thing that's important to you."

Name begins with a *J* . . .

Photographing sea turtles . . .

That doesn't make sense. A man with a camera in a place with sea turtles. I don't know anybody like that.

Until I realize that I do.

JONAH IS A photographer I met at capoeira. Though I resolved early on that I wouldn't "meet someone" in capoeira (it was my sanctuary from looking for love), I could consider changing my policy for Jonah. Just for Jonah. Jonah with a *J*. Jonah has hazel eyes and black-framed glasses, a wardrobe's worth of plaid shirts, and the straightest, whitest teeth I've ever seen because his father is a dentist.

The problem with Jonah, though, is that he often speaks of his future wife. All our capoeira friends know about her, a woman who left him and left the country. For months he's insisted they're getting back together, which they did, but she hasn't returned. Now he insists she's coming back. But if someone leaves you and then, from a distance, reels you back with apologies and promises of a fresh start, it can't end well, can it? The Profiler would call that a negative sign.

But the sea turtle revelation has convinced me. This was too specific to be a coincidence. Our group of capoeira friends—Jonah included—have plans to attend another mutual capoeira friend's wedding in Puerto Rico before I am supposed to leave for China. We've rented an apartment near the five-star resort where she is getting married. There are sea turtles in Puerto Rico, and Jonah will photograph them because he takes pictures of everything. The prophecy will practically fulfill itself.

When the China job suddenly falls through, I'm convinced fate had a hand. The reader's prediction has become more specific than ever, too precise to ignore.

I send my friend, the bride, to a session with the reader as a bachelorette present. My friend, an accomplished executive, is more rational than I, but she is also a good friend, not the type to tell me I'm insane and she'd rather have the champagne flutes. She accepts my gift, scheduling her date with divination mere days before she will leave for her tropical paradise wedding. I don't know what questions she brings to the appointment. I'm too concerned with my new Sea Turtle Prince Jonah to ask.

THE RESORT OCCUPIES 483 acres of former coconut plantation and is a Certified Gold Audubon Signature Sanctuary, which means the inevitability of sea turtles on its fine sand, my fate held in a Nikon D7000 over their nests. It's a landscape of winding roads, lush vegetation, and palm trees bearing signs that read IGUANA CROSSING.

Iguanas are everywhere. No sea turtles.

In the morning, we see the bride's father at the alfresco restaurant. He plans to hike in the jungle and swim in the ocean before the evening ceremony. There's a room reserved for wedding guests staying elsewhere to rest and get refreshed. The group of friends—minus the bride, who has hair and makeup appointments—heads to the pool.

An iguana lazes in the poolside shrubbery. As if to mock the sea turtle prediction, Jonah fetches his camera and starts snapping away while I try to figure out how to lure him to the beach, where the sea turtles will be.

He waves me over from the other end of the pool. "Come look at this!"

"What is it?"

"This other iguana," he says.

I approach where he stands taking pictures of a second iguana. It is some kind of aquatic iguana with a spiky crest, like a marine iguana, the kind only known to exist in the Galapagos. This iguana goes for a swim in the pool as if it were a guest at the resort. Jonah snaps more pictures.

"We should go in soon, get ready," he says.

"Yes, but please just come down to the beach first," I say, hoping to nudge fate along, sea turtle induction.

"Okay."

While this is happening, some lobbyists at the resort for a political fundraiser spot something odd-sized floating in the shallow water. A suitcase? A dolphin?

Jonah and I make our way down the path toward the ocean, until we are stopped by the groom. His face is pale. Scenarios flash through my mind: someone has come to the resort to assassinate a politician, or a dangerous and estranged distant relative has shown up—real telenovela stuff. These absurd thoughts are abandoned as he speaks, replaced by the knowledge of something more horrifying. There is a body on the beach, he says. They think it's her father, he says.

It can't be, I say. We just saw him at breakfast. What I keep to myself: The tarot reader would have called it. She would have told the bride to keep her father out of the water. It's no secret that we live our daily lives as if we're protected from tragedy. That's survival. A wedding adds another coat of armor to this imaginary shield. Fathers don't die at weddings two hours before they're supposed to walk their daughters down the aisle. That wouldn't happen, I tell Jonah, as if there's a contract with the realm of possibility that bans such a coincidence. On the beach, confused lobbyists huddle around a mass covered by what appears to be a hotel sheet.

REMEMBER SCHROEDINGER'S CAT? The paradoxical thought experiment about the cat in the box that's somehow alive and dead at the same time? I'm no physicist, but it's always fascinated me. The cat is in a box with a Geiger counter, a bottle of poison, a hammer, and some radioactive substance. When the radioactive substance decays, the Geiger counter triggers the hammer to break the bottle, and the poison kills the cat. Until the box is opened, though, it is unknown whether the cat is dead or alive. There is no way to predict when or if the radioactive decay—a random process—has occurred. So the cat is both living and dead until the box is opened.

Schroedinger's purpose was to illustrate how, in a physical system, you cannot say what something is doing until it is observed. In the many-worlds interpretation, in one universe the boxed cat might be dead, while in another, parallel universe it might live on. It suggests that much exists beyond the boundaries our limited perception. It's the same reason I'm addicted to the tarot reader.

Before the sheet is lifted, could the body underneath be simultaneously father and not-father? Can fathers be both dead and alive, until observed?

MY FATHER DOESN'T drink anymore because he drank so much he can never drink again. In that case, it was expected or should have been, but even though I knew about his alcoholism, heard reports from his brother that my father did not leave the apartment anymore or let anyone in, I didn't believe his death was coming. I never observed my own father's body. The news came via long-distance phone call, the funeral fast, hidden, abroad—the brother arranging and completing it all before I had time to book a flight. I've never been to his grave. So could he still be out there, wandering, estranged? Is it any wonder I long to believe in magic?

IN THIS CASE it does not remain a mystery for long. The body did belong to him. Now it belongs to her, the bride, one of my closest friends. Like me, she's an only child. Unlike me, she doesn't have an overbearing mother—she lost her mother when she was younger. Instead of being walked down the aisle, she is responsible for arranging the body's removal from the beach before her wedding, dealing with the morgue in this bureaucratically unsound island paradise. She paces alongside the gathered crowd, talking into a cell phone. We have similar reactions in crisis situations, she and I: we deal, at first, by taking action. Doing what must be done. A member of the resort staff wraps bright yellow tape around some palm trees.

"Maybe the body is fine," someone says. "Maybe they're just giving it some air."

Everyone wants to help, but there isn't anything to do. Somebody says her father was getting in a last swim before going inside to change.

It's difficult to align all this with the kind of reality I wish for, the kind with divine seers, predictability, certainty: the kind that drives me to the by-referral-only tarot reader. Why didn't she warn my friend?

Didn't the tarot reader see such a huge tragedy coming, of all things? If she did, she covered it up, and if she didn't—either way, my reliance on her is called into question. Jonah didn't photograph sea turtles anyway. The whole sea turtle thing is suddenly ridiculous and obscene. How had we just been sitting on the pool patio, drinking mojitos?

IN THE HOTEL room, we wait to hear about the wedding. This is like waiting in an airport for news of a possibly cancelled flight. We down mixed drinks, rum with minibar Diet Cokes. When the unbelievable and unreal happens, it brings all that is believable and real into question. This undermines my deep-seated desire to believe things happen for a reason, even though I don't really believe this at all. It's a crisis of faith without the faith.

Jonah and I play backgammon on my phone. Everyone talks about fathers. We relate what we experience back to prior experience. Something to anchor to, any anchor. I'm facing down my own father-lessness. It's not that I even want to tell another story about love and death and faith, but not having a choice in our stories seems part of the point.

One father disappears, another washes up on the shore of the shallowest sea. I have never told my friends the story of my father. We can be so close yet unaware of these person-defining facts. Jonah is predictable. He is stable. His father is a dentist.

"Want to hear something dumb?" I say as Jonah presses the phone screen for a digital dice roll. "I go to a tarot reader sometimes. A by-referral-only tarot reader. I actually believe the things she tells me, like that I'm going to marry a guy who I'll see taking pictures of sea turtles. Isn't that absurd?"

"Ridiculous," he agrees.

"Yes, exactly. Ridiculous."

I feel guilty for trashing my beloved tarot reader who has been right about so many things over the years. I instantly regret revealing the prophecy, as now I've messed with it, which has altered the natural course of events. It won't happen. But the reader betrayed me. She invented sea turtle photography and my destiny with Jonah and she didn't tell our friend to keep her father out of the ocean.

We take turns checking on the bride in her suite. She looks beautiful. The wedding will happen—we're all here, it's what he would have wanted. She is on the phone with the morgue. His body has not yet been taken. She is placed on hold. It starts to rain.

"I wonder if it's raining on my father," she says.

Yes, we are a lot alike, my friend and I.

THE WEDDING PROCEEDS. One of the groom's uncles steps into the role of father, walking the bride down the aisle. Vows recited. What can we do when tragedy is contained within a celebration but forge ahead? At the reception, I crunch a chip loaded with the most incredible tuna tartare I've ever tasted. Champagne is poured. The humid tropical air smells of flowers and feels good on my skin. My senses are heightened. I'm awake to every sensation, every sound. I dance with Jonah. At one point I move in to kiss him. I'd say facing down the finite nature of existence made me bold, but it was the Veuve Clicquot. He stops me.

"I'm sorry," he says. "It's not going to happen."

"Why not?"

The DJ spins a Latin pop track. Jonah speaks into my ear of the girl who's coming back to him.

"I had a dream once that I married her. This may sound weird, or maybe not given what you told me earlier, but I've always had prophetic dreams. I don't know how to describe it to you. It's not really something I can explain."

"What if you're wrong?"

"I'm going there next week, bringing her back to New York. But don't worry, you still have your sea turtle man coming up."

I want to sink into that marble floor. First of all, in the face of death I am still preoccupied with love. Secondly, a prophecy is only useful when it tells you what you want to hear.

AT THE AIRPORT, hungover and awaiting my flight home, I listen to the tarot reader's recording in hopes that it might somehow provide comfort, that there might be a clue that my sea turtle man is still out there. I fast-forward to the part about sea turtles and realize I made a mistake. She doesn't say sea turtles. She never said sea turtles. I don't know where I got sea turtles. She names an entirely different animal: marine iguanas.

That resort is a hotbed of iguanas. If I hadn't misheard, if I'd known the whole time he was taking pictures of iguanas, would I have experienced a transcendent moment of recognition that I did not because of my error? I check Jonah's photography blog. It is already plastered with pictures of iguanas. Fate got me on this one. It was real all along, and I can't tell Jonah he fulfilled the prophecy after all. He's already gone. I've mistaken the force of my will, again, for the magic of fate. But then another thing arises. On this closer listen, it becomes evident that the tarot reader was only speaking metaphorically anyway. She'd meant that I would encounter my future husband on my travels that summer in an unexpected way. Marine iguana photography was only an example, a stand-in for randomness. Now I wonder if the question isn't about whether I believe or not, but whether she can be right and wrong at the same time.

ONCE I READ about the strangest coincidences ever known. One was a cab driver in Jamaica who hit and killed a guy on a moped in an intersection, and exactly one year later, in the same intersection, with the same passenger in his cab, he hit and killed the guy's brother, who was riding the same moped.

SOME MEMBERS OF the group of friends are supposed to go to Santa Cruz, California, for the capoeira batizado of our academy's West Coast outpost. We cancel our flights as soon as we are back in New York, so we can attend the funeral of the bride's father. In my early thirties, it's my first—the viewing, tossing handfuls of dirt into the grave. I thought

I'd missed out on closure by not having gotten to my father's funeral, but the ritual doesn't provide closure, at least not for me. You know what does? Research. Facts. I need to follow breadcrumb paths toward some illusion of a deeper understanding, even if it does have to be tinted, to some extent, with dabbling in magic. I need to know: If she's such an elite tarot card reader, why did she not see it? Or did she see it and not say?

I ASK THE bride if I can listen to her session recording. "I need to know what she saw." My friend sends over the audio file. I'm surprised that one of her first questions is, "Will my father's health be good over the next year?"

The reader draws some cards and points out the star and the tower. "Sometimes he doesn't address issues with you the way he should," she tells my friend. "He doesn't take care of himself the way he should. Your dad's an interesting guy. There may be something that happens that throws him a bit out of balance."

What I wonder most is why my friend chose this question in the first place.

She asks about the wedding.

"The death card," the reader says, "the death of bishops and kings. There is something on the horizon. It's like why didn't that show up?"

Is she talking to herself? Or hiding something?

I CALL THE by-referral-only tarot reader, this time not to make an appointment, but to find out what happened. I tell her nothing about the bride's father. My intent is twofold: I don't want to hurt her by coming across as accusing her of having been wrong and demanding an answer. I also want to try to uncover, purely, if she was hiding what she saw, and, if so, why.

"What can be seen, in terms of death, in your line of work?" I ask. "Can you see if someone is going to die? And is it mandatory to tell the client, or would you not do that? Like, a code of professional conduct?"

The by-referral-only tarot card reader is oblique. "The universe tells you what you need to know," she says. "You don't ask about something you don't want to know."

How does she know what or how much someone really wants to know? If she'd issued a warning, would my friend have kept her father out of the ocean? Away from the wedding? Maybe his death at that moment was inevitable no matter where he was. My mind spirals, a marine iguana eating its own tail.

A few days later, the bride and I drive through Brooklyn in her father's SUV, now her SUV. A plaque on the bumper reads, FISH NOW, WORK LATER.

"Maybe she didn't know, but you had some idea," I say.

"How so?"

"Why did you choose that question?"

Maybe we all have to be our own by-referral-only tarot readers, making our own calls about our own marine iguanas.

I ARRIVE ON the patio of our favorite neighborhood bar, crowded with summertime revelers. The group of friends sits with takeout tacos and pitchers of beer. Jonah holds up a photograph on his phone. It is a marine iguana. Not the fake Puerto Rico pool kind, but the majestic, colorful, huge, and real Galápagos kind. I walk in on Jonah showing this photograph to the table.

"Who took this?" I ask.

"My father," he says, "just got back from a tour of the Galápagos."

When not working on teeth, Jonah's father is also a photographer. This is his picture. Jonah mentions that he, too, would like to travel to the Galápagos to photograph these strange, majestic beasts. That the pool iguana in Puerto Rico was just a warm-up for the real thing. He's joking and my head is swimming. He doesn't know about my mistake. The false sea turtles. There may still be hope. Somewhere inside this marine iguana hall of mirrors, I'm trying to figure out what to make of the signs but have gotten no closer.

THINGS THAT CAN be known:

The marine iguanas lie on salty Galápagos rocks.

The pool iguana swims in Puerto Rico, permanent guest of the five-star resort.

The fathers are underground. Or they are dentists.

The by-referral-only tarot card reader sits six stories up in her studio a mile away, reading cards.

Somewhere, sea turtles lay eggs in the sand.

I STILL BELIEVE, and still I don't.

THERE'S A LINK between love and death and story, something to do with urgency. Isn't there a bright, flashing urgency to it all, knowing all of this could be gone in an instant? The time of the marine iguana prediction would be the last I'd see the by-referral-only tarot reader. My own father is a memory. It is easier to conduct daily life as if death is a question, a rare condition, as if there are odds it won't happen. Fathers, lobbyists, sea turtles . . . You preserve these bugs in the amber of moments.

Photographer of all photographers Annie Leibovitz said, "Things happen all the time that are unexpected, uncontrolled, even magical. The work prepares you for that moment. Suddenly the clouds roll in and the soft light you longed for appears."

JONAH FLIES TO visit the woman who left him. If he is in fact marine iguana man, I'm in for a long wait. I leave the city again, to a capoeira retreat in Ithaca. I don't consider a short trip upstate to be in the realm of "summer travels," but if I'd been in China, I would not have come here. I don't think about this though. No one here is photographing marine iguanas or sea turtles, nor is there any marine life around at all, other than some plain fish in a lake. Months later, I'm in California, and I check Twitter and see Jonah got married to the woman he brought back, just as he dreamed he would. At least someone's prophecy was right.

THE PROFILER SELECTS

AFTER DECIDING THAT my mother would have to approve any man I was contemplating a relationship with, I wrote a piece about her profiling "powers," ending with my mother and I debating the merits of JDate. I sent the story to the editor of the Modern Love column in the *New York Times*, who responded with an acceptance.

The Sunday the article was slated to run, I was on a weekend capoeira retreat in Ithaca, where Foca and Rouxinol had moved after closing their Brooklyn capoeira academy. It would be a good distraction, I thought. I was already queasy about imagined mocking reactions to the idea of a woman in her thirties whose judgment in romantic partners was so terrible that she needed her overbearing mother to screen men. I had nothing to lose . . . except my dignity. I spent the weekend with old friends and made a new one, the capoeira instructor from our group's sister academy in Santa Cruz, California. His apelido was Melão–melon—because of his bald head. I recognized him because he'd come to Brooklyn for our batizados before, but when I bounded over and cheerfully greeted him I realized he had no idea who I, a beginner, was.

"So what brings you all the way here?" I asked.

"I usually go to Brazil every summer," he said. He was a special-education elementary school teacher, so he had summers off. "But I was visiting my girlfriend in L.A. and broke up a dogfight at her house. I got bit."

He showed me the scar on his arm, still red and fresh.

"My stitches came out the day I was supposed to get on the plane for Brazil. I cancelled my trip. But when the stitches came out I was fine so I'm here instead." I was sorry he got bit but grateful for the coincidence, as that weekend he taught me a new technique for learning a front-walk-over acrobatic move that had eluded me for the last two years.

Next thing I knew it was Sunday and my friends were stopping at a gas station for gas but also to pick up a copy of the newspaper with my article in it. They wanted me to read it aloud on the ride back to the city. They did laugh at the woman whose judgment in romantic partners was so terrible that she needed her overbearing mother to screen men, but I found I wasn't embarrassed or ashamed. It was like the stitches came out and there would be a scar but I found my arm was fine. The "me" in the article, a characterization of my former self, wasn't only someone I could laugh at too, but someone I'd learned from. I even kind of liked her overbearing mother.

In the week that followed, a few of the requisite cutting messages that go along with publishing any personal essay did arrive, but the article also received some feedback that struck my mother and me: "This mother," a reader wrote in, "has been awfully good at pointing out what's wrong with the guys her daughter is choosing, but what has she really done to help her daughter find someone who's right?"

"What if I started a blog," my mother suggested, "to help you find the right man? If any guys write after reading your article, you can direct them to me for screening."

I considered her suggestion, which seemed to be entirely serious. I already knew I would do it. It was very Old World, the notion of mother as matchmaker. And in our current culture, absurd. Possibly ridiculous. I loved it. But primarily, I had hit an all-time low in my quest for the right love. I'm not pessimistic by nature, but I was beginning to feel, if not pessimistic about it, at least resigned. It wasn't fun. I needed to shake things up. It wasn't desperation but rather a new state of mind in which I was open to new possibilities, even if it meant completely altering the way I had viewed my mother for the entirety of my conscious existence. If The Big Mom In The Sky saw all, maybe she could spot the right man for me down here on Earth. Giving up control felt not defeating but adventur-ous. I was curious to see what would happen if she actually conducted an official search for profiling candidates. She was smart and good at her job. What possibilities might turn up if I embraced her help rather than resisting it? It involved reframing for her, too: rather than simply axing the men in my path, she would use her "superpower" for good—rather than weeding out the ones who were wrong, she would embark on a pro-active search to find one who was right. It could be good for her, too. For the first time, I was giving my mother exactly what she wanted: complete control. And I'd go along for the ride.

"I've made bad decisions," I said. "You make them for me. Let's see if you do a better job."

WHEN SHE VISITED a couple days later, I showed her my Tumblr account and walked her through setting up a blog: http://theprofilerselects.tumblr.com was born.

"Did you learn how to do this in school?" she asked.

It was adorable. I wanted to hug her. It was the cutest thing she'd ever said.

"No, Mom. They don't teach this in school."

She came up with the descriptions and application qualifications: "potential suitors" needed to be intelligent, kind, financially solvent, energetic, and in possession of a valid passport. She requested a writing sample and a photo.

THAT WEEK, A solid handful of men did actually email me directly after doing some online sleuthing. They reported that maybe they were "the one," if I'd be willing to meet them. I wasn't going to fly away to the farmer in Ireland, but there were a few local men whose messages I passed along to my mother. She invited them to formally apply.

I posted a link to her blog and directed applicants there. I thought even the interested men might balk at a formal application process, but to my surprise, they started rolling in. My mother selected three for me to go on dates with: a former doctor who stopped practicing medicine to start his own hedge fund, an international composer who was closer to my mother's age than mine, and a young diplomat who specialized in conflict mitigation for tribal leaders in war-torn regions. They were impressive on paper, and I was impressed with my mother. She wasn't just The Profiler now, telling me I was making wrong decisions. She'd taken on a more active, positive role: as a diplomatchmaker. After years of serial monogamy, guided by her professional skill at quick assessments, I started dating.

PROFILER CANDIDATE #1
Perfect on Paper: The Hedge Fund Doctor
He's smart and motivated, The Profiler said, and I agreed. We had a good email rapport, a promising sign.

He asked me to meet at a fancy restaurant near Gramercy Park. It was a little stuffy, and I shifted uncomfortably in my plush velvet seat, but The Doctor was kind. He showed me pictures of his artwork. I understood why he was "quite proud" of his pieces: they were stunning. He was so intelligent, thoughtful, and interested in me—but. Of course there was a "but." There wasn't chemistry. I hung out all night talking with him, but couldn't imagine us kissing.

Why not? I asked myself over and over. He was everything: warm, kind, intelligent, fun to be around, a great conversationalist, successful, artistic. Yes, he was all of those things . . . and still, there just wasn't the physical attraction. *Damn it*, I thought as I returned to the Union Square subway after the date.

I wouldn't tell my mother this next part:

On the subway platform, I texted Andy, my ex who had not yet left for his Burning Man–fueled adventure and was still in the city. We met later, at a bar in Brooklyn. Coming from The Hedge Fund Doctor, I could understand The Profiler's statement that Andy wasn't right for me, but there was undeniable chemistry. I went home with Andy, and in the morning I walked to my apartment thinking about what makes for the right partnership. I hadn't broken it down before. I'd just pursued feelings. That hadn't worked. But love couldn't be approached entirely from a logical stance, either.

PROFILER CANDIDATE #2
Perfect for Her: The Old Composer

My second date was The Old Composer, a divorced man with salt-and-pepper hair. He wasn't elderly, but he had a kid my age, which set him at a disadvantage even though he appeared far younger than his years. We met at a wine bar in the West Village that I'd picked out. Over sauvignon blanc and appetizers, he told me of his travels throughout Asia and Europe, his composing work, and his previous life with his ex-wife. I wanted to go home and take a bubble bath. He wanted to go to a diner for cheesecake and coffee. I ordered pie and drank coffee, fantasizing about the bubble bath I would take when I got home. When I told him he should meet my mother, he seemed surprised. But a few days later he emailed her. She said he would meet her sometime when they could be in the same city.

PROFILER CANDIDATE #3
Just Plain Perfect: The Exciting Young Diplomat

It seemed the third time might really be a charm: the application from the man my mother dubbed "the Exciting Young Diplomat" was "energetic, upbeat, fun," she wrote. He didn't just have the requisite passport. He held a diplomatic one.

THE DIPLOMAT WAS coming up from D.C. for a weekend, staying in Fort Greene, and wanted to get together on Friday.

For our brunch date, I biked over to Fort Greene. As I was locking my bicycle, I spotted him waiting on a bench outside the restaurant. He was handsome in a chiseled way. He exuded the air of quiet confidence a conflict mitigator for tribal leaders in war-torn regions probably should. I walked up to him and introduced myself, and we hugged hello. I liked his vibe, mellow but in control. We were the same age. He was even better looking up close, when I could see his blue eyes. I became nervous, but his calm nature put me at ease. (Made sense, he put tense people at ease for a living.) As we ate, conversation flowed. We'd both dabbled in film industry jobs before going on to other careers—I to writing, he to the Georgetown School of Foreign Service. I left our lively brunch date, biked home in the warm springtime sun, and promptly called my mother.

"You were right!" I said exuberantly into her voicemail. "Profiling worked."

I would happily date The Diplomat. How cool was *that* "how we met" story: he was the last of my three Profiler-arranged dates! I didn't have to meet anyone else after him! It was kismet!

Except . . . he never called.

I wrote to The Profiler about this quandary. She said, "Maybe he'll write in a day or two."

Only he didn't write in a day or two. Or three or four or five. A week later, I received one Facebook message. He'd been following The Profiler's blog, which had been updated with the story of our "positive" first "get-together."

He wrote: "Oh boy, mom's on a roll. The interwebs will never be the same. I'll holler next time I'm coming up."

Maybe he just never came back to New York. Maybe Mom's blog scared him off. Most likely he just wasn't interested.

"With the right one it will go both ways," The Profiler said. "He had potential, but I can't predict his actions."

HOW COULD WE drum up more candidates? While I'd been enmeshed in quick-fire dating, momentum had died down. Applications had dried up. How to solicit more men? My mother and I weren't sure. We had finally hit on something we could do together, a project we bonded over, and it seemed to have ended before it could pick up enough momentum. The Profiler hadn't found me the one, but I was grateful: I wouldn't have met any of these three interesting, accomplished men without her. Three delicious meals. Three engaging conversations. Three chances at breaking out of my comfort zone.

My mother was surprisingly accepting that none of the men she'd approved turned out to be the one. Was she trusting my judgment? Our conversations in the aftermath of our project made me realize that the real reward wasn't the dating, but an unanticipated side effect of collaborating with my mother: something had shifted between The Profiler and me. Where we used to fall into an argument, we now had an exchange. I asked for her feedback, and she listened to my needs. We may not have found me a new relationship, but we came out of the journey with a better version of our own. Or at least a reprieve before it would resurface again in a different form.

A note from the desk of

THE PROFILER

NONE OF THE respondents to the blog were the "perfect" match for Liza. But they all possessed admirable, worthy traits, talents, and professions. They had my approval to meet Liza. Then, it was over to her for the dating experience, her reactions to the suitors, and theirs to her.

After retiring from the Foreign Service, in my new role as The Profiler, I put my experiences to the test in a new way to find a good match for my daughter. Since the suitors did not appear in person the way the visa applicants in the consular section did, I could not rely on an actual interview with verbal communication, gestures, and body language. Adapting my techniques to assess men submitting requests via the blog, I first looked at their photos, then at the content of their messages—their jobs, their interests, and how they expressed themselves in writing. You can tell a lot about someone from a photo. Look at the eyes, face, clothes. Long hair and tattoos, or clean cut? Smiling or serious?

How did they write? All of them wrote very well—bright, clever, good use of language. Good jobs, good experiences, and positive vibes from what and how they wrote. I gave a thumbs-up to The Doctor and The Diplomat right away, but was leery about the composer, more than twenty-two years older than Liza. Since he was accomplished, talented, well traveled, multilingual, and divorced, I agreed she could meet him for coffee. But I did alert him first to my concerns with the age difference.

A lot of singles are impatient and want a Hollywood romance on the first meeting. But don't dismiss a date for silly reasons: wrong height, hair, etc. I told Liza to give these applicants a chance. Liza insisted that both physical attraction and inner qualities were important. I thought if the guy had good qualities, even if the attraction wasn't there initially, she could fall in love over time. I was rooting for The Doctor, but she didn't feel the "spark" with him. The Diplomat? Interesting job and a good sense of humor! He sounded great, too. And when they met, she liked him. But no go. He apparently wasn't interested in her. The Old Composer? Ironically, Liza thought he was perfect—for me. I agreed. We emailed, but I guess I'm too close to his age to be of interest.

It's not easy to find Mr. Right. I'm still searching. Let me know if you come across a man in his sixties, retired, enjoys travel, financially sound . . .

THE SKEPTIC
AND THE VISION
BOARD PARTY

ONE COLD, DARK New York City night during a cold, dark time, a Paperless Post invitation arrived in my inbox.

NEW AGE KASSI HERE.

JOIN ME FOR A

VISION BOARD PARTY

FRIDAY FEBRUARY 24th, 2012

7.30pm–MIDNIGHT

It continued:

The vision boards will project our incredible futures . . . A Pulitzer? Hotter sex? Bicoastal living? Throughout the next few years, it'll probably manifest.

I'll provide poster board, magazines, glue, and a printer.

TRUE STORY: I wrote myself fake acceptance letters from Columbia and the New York Times. Then I got real ones. New Age Kassi believes in the power of visions.

This was how the Kassi I knew, then just plain Kassi, attained what became her perpetual moniker. Until the arrival of that invitation, I hadn't known that Kassi Underwood—author of a gorgeous book then in progress about depoliticizing abortion, whip-smart professor whose personal style was more Saks than Sedona—had anything to do with the realm of crystals, chakras, and unicorns. I double-checked the contact info on the invite. What *The Secret*–espousing fluffy rainbow fiend had possessed my rational friend?

When it comes to the occult, faith, and the mystical, I'm skeptical of it all, but it's more fun to think that it might be real than to live in a world devoid of signs and magic.

To inch toward true belief, I require *some* evidence. But vision boards—let's just say vision boards were where I drew the line. They were dumb. The "law of attraction" was pure conjecture. Thinking you could get what you wanted by gluing some strips of paper to a board was absurd. And whereas tarot readers and psychoanalysts see clients of every gender, the idea of vision boarding as something women do angered me. It painted us as frivolous: while men are out there achieving their goals through action, women need to invoke the divine by gluing paper cutouts on construction paper and hoping it will work, because that's how limited our likelihood of achieving our ambitions is (and I want to say especially in the male-dominated field of "serious" literature, but isn't it all fields, still?).

New Age Kassi had invited only women—making posters over a few hours with snacks and wine sounded innocuous at worst, and it was probably intended as a "sisterhood" thing, not in the more negative light in which I saw the gender aspect, but I still couldn't get over the idea of vision boards as a naïve romantic comedy cliché. I wondered if we ladies were more likely to believe in something that removes agency, rather than accepting the reality that the only way to achieve goals is via dedication and hard work. I imagined some kind of slogan: Real Men Don't Make Vision Boards. (Except for 50 Cent, who advocated for them in an interview.)

Though I could simply have clicked Will Not Attend, I told New Age Kassi I was going to be out of town so I wouldn't be tempted to say what I really thought they could do with those vision boards.

A few months after the vision board party, New Age Kassi and I were sitting in a nail salon near the university where we both taught. I asked how her book was going.

"I found an agent," she said. "Actually, he found me. He emailed me out of the blue after reading an article I wrote, wanting to represent me."

"That's amazing."

She'd also connected with the man of her dreams, down to his being six foot two. (They would soon be engaged.)

I commented on how much success New Age Kassi had met with since I'd last seen her.

"Vision boards, baby," she said.

My skepticism shifted—albeit slightly—to curiosity. All of the good things that were happening were, coincidentally or not, related to images she'd glued on her vision board at the party I'd refused to attend. More was to come: besides the board's career and love sections, she had pasted the word "tour" and city names. She was invited on a yearlong national storytelling tour that brought her to the very places on her board. She had posted the words "comedy's heavy hitters," and got to read a humor piece she wrote at an event with Sarah Silverman, Amy Schumer, and Lizz Winstead. The kicker: she sold her book.

I told New Age Kassi that, in retribution for my closed-mindedness, not only would I make a vision board, I would host the next vision board party myself.

"Go big. Put everything you want on your vision board," she advised, "because you never know what is attainable."

I INVITED MEN to my vision board party, curious if any would come. Of the fifteen people attending Vision Board Sunday at my Brooklyn apartment, four of them were men. One, Matthew Hutson, is the author of a book with the subtitle *How Irrational Beliefs Keep Us Happy, Healthy, and Sane,* and also holds a degree in cognitive neuroscience from Brown University. I was hopeful he could help lend his scientific perspective to this vision board business. In his book, Hutson quotes some gems that applied to my predicament, such as a story about the physicist Niels Bohr responding to a friend's inquiry about how he, a scientist, could ascribe to superstitious nonsense (Bohr had a horseshoe above his door).

"Oh, I don't believe in it," Bohr responded. "But I am told it works even if you don't." The psychologist Carol Nemeroff, who has studied magical thinking extensively, told Hutson that "the answer for many people, especially with regard to magic, is, 'Most of me doesn't believe, but some of me does.'"

We sat on the floor surrounded by magazines, glue sticks, scissors, construction paper boards, and mimosas. Absurd or not, I was doing it, and it was forcing me to think about what I wanted most: to live at least a few months per year in California (I loved palm trees, loathed winter, and wanted to be able to wear flip-flops year round, if I chose); find a publisher for my marriage memoir; and travel to Brazil again for capoeira. I began thumbing through the magazines and cutting out pictures and phrases that fit with my dreams: an image of a house and text that read "Inspired Acre of Heaven," "The next level thanks to inspiration," "dedication," and "beautiful scenery," and for the book section: "Bold Paperback Nonfiction," "Author Tour," and "Patience Pays Off." I added palm trees, a cliff overlooking the ocean, and a piece on Brazil and capoeira I (coincidentally?) found intact in a *Vogue* travel spread.

Which reminded me:

Rafael, a Brazilian friend I was hosting for a weeklong capoeira event, was slated to arrive that evening. I was embarrassed that we might not be done with the vision boards by then and he would see what resembled kindergarten art projects.

Though I felt ridiculous using art supplies I hadn't picked up since childhood to attempt to summon what I most wanted into reality, I admired all the other vision boards, fascinated to see my friends' goals and dreams laid out in such an easily digestible format. I didn't finish mine. When Rafael arrived, torn-up magazines, glue, and scissors were everywhere. I explained the concept of vision boards. He didn't eye-roll at "these crazy Americans." He nodded as if he understood. Was everyone more open to this than me?

After the party, I set out to finish my board. Rafael surveyed my nearly complete work: the capoeira photo spread, book publishers, palm trees and beach views. I had, for no conscious reason, attached a string of Tibetan flags over the California section. They had arrived in a mailed donation request.

"You no want mans?" Rafael asked.

I realized he meant I had put no love section on my board. The only thing cheesier than a vision board was a love section on a vision board.

"A man." I corrected him, but he was the one who had corrected me: of course I wanted love. So far, I hadn't found good candidates. Rafael, who is married, said something about how everybody needs love, so I caved, cutting out a picture of a pleasant-seeming man carrying a box. It wouldn't be so bad if a handsome, smart, adorable "mans" showed up. Especially if what's inside the box is new shoes. I pasted him down next to a palm tree, along with the word "love" and a woman with two children creating "an outdoor oasis for her family."

"There," I said. "Done."

I stashed the vision board on my desk. It was too humiliating to display. I'd figure out what to do with it later. The capoeira week with visitors from Brazil and across the country was about to begin.

ON THE THURSDAY of capoeira week, I had a morning meeting in Manhattan and offered to take the visitors to the High Line. When I got there, Melão, the instructor from California, was the only one who showed up.

On the High Line, I told him about the aftermath of the Profiler article and the dates. How Rafael had talked me into a love section on the vision board, and how silly I still thought vision boards were. Since Melão lived in Santa Cruz—where Buddha statues sit in the succulent gardens outside of people's homes, and everyone and their grandmother has a vision board—he understood. He talked about his own relationship, which I'd idealized after seeing a photograph of one of their camping trips on Facebook. I'd been wrong. There was trouble in paradise.

"I'm in the process of breaking up with her," he said.

They had started dating when they were twenty-five. The previous winter, when they were in their early thirties, she had moved six hours away to go to graduate school. They traded weekend visits, but with distance he was realizing that while he loved her, he wasn't going to propose. They were almost right for each other. He'd been anguishing for a while over the "almost."

"Thanks for putting up with me all day," Melão said as we arrived at the capoeira academy that evening for class.

SPENDING MORE TIME with Melão that week, I learned he was smart, funny, kind, and, like the man standing beside a palm tree on my vision board, a sweet and generous spirit.

Rafael said, "You two would be perfect."

"He has a girlfriend."

"I no like them together. You and him, perfect."

"It's a good sign, though," I told my friend Pinguinha in the parking lot of her apartment building the next day. "It means there must be others like him out there."

"Let's go through his Facebook friends," Pinguinha said. "If he's that great he must know others who are like him. We can look through his list of friends and meet them when we go to the batizado in Santa Cruz."

I agreed to profile his Facebook friends, but felt a little bit sad about it.

ON SATURDAY NIGHT, the mestre from Santa Cruz, a Brazilian who also headlines a band called SambaDá, was playing a show at SOB's (Sounds of Brazil), a venue in the West Village. Melão and I were dancing. It was easier not to pay attention to sexual tension while walking the High Line and the busy streets of Brooklyn. It's much harder when gyrationally dancing to the cheesy Brazilian hit "Ai Se Eu Te Pego."

"I think I have to stop dancing with you now," he said, voicing my own feelings. I went to the other side of the club to reconvene with my friends, but to my surprise he showed back up and we kept right on dancing.

We kissed on the subway to Brooklyn and walked back to the mutual friend's apartment where Melão was staying. As with the dancing, we kept kissing, but stayed in the realm of, as Melão would later phrase it, "chaste." Mostly, we talked for the rest of the night on the air mattress on the floor of our friend's spare room.

"What's one word you'd use to describe your reactions to most situations in life?" I asked him, thinking of my own: "amusement."

"Amusement," he said right away.

It was past noon on Sunday when we finally got up. I was certain this perfect night was a freak accident, that Melão would go back, visit his girlfriend in L.A., tell her everything, apologize profusely, and propose. This—the one-night, *Before Sunrise*-style connection—is the kind of thing people in long-term relationships have when they are in a moment of crisis. A fleeting, momentary connection with a "what could have been" person. Then they go get married and have babies with the long-term partner they were having the crisis about. I believed this to the point that when Melão hugged me in front of our capoeira friend in the kitchen, I became embarrassed and pulled away.

I picked up my phone to tons of missed calls and voicemails from my mother. We had plans to go to a reading I was giving in Westchester that day, and had to catch a train at Grand Central soon if we were going to make it. The reading was of an essay about my father. I didn't really want to go read it out loud to a room full of strangers but had committed to the event. I replied to my mother that I would be on my way soon.

"Whenever there's some guy, you'll just abandon your mother," she said when I walked in. "The Profiler does not approve."

"Relax, Mom. Let's go."

WHEN I LEFT on Monday—the first of October—for the Thurber House in Columbus, Ohio, for a month-long writing residency, the vision board I'd made a week and a day earlier couldn't have been further from my mind.

Then strange things started happening. While I was in Columbus, my six-years-in-the-making marriage memoir found a publisher. The same week, Melão told me he'd called his girlfriend on the drive home from the airport. Instead of getting engaged as I'd suspected, they had ended it. We started texting and then talking on Skype. He made plans to visit for a four-day-long first date in Columbus.

At the old writing desk downstairs in the Thurber House museum, where I sometimes wrote in front of afternoon visitors like a living installation, I changed his name from Melão to Jason in my phone, a momentous occasion for people who introduce themselves by made-up capoeira apelidos. Only then did I realize: I'd met him on my summer travels. And his real name begins with a *J*.

Soon, it looked as though the vision board had become a portal I'd stepped through. (Note to self: must write Charlie Kaufman–esque movie in which this happens.) The marriage memoir found its own way, and I was pleased with its reception.

After all the wrong decisions, making the right one was oddly easy. And here I am in Santa Cruz, California. This is what you might call a "New Agey" place. Vision boarding was one of the first activities a new friend suggested we do together, after surfboarding. Tibetan prayer flags are everywhere: hanging from my neighbors' front porches, my friend's balcony, the redwood forest. The cliff above the sea resembles the beachside city's landscape, and our house, the "acre of heaven." The Perfect Mans and I traveled to Brazil and played capoeira. Travel well together? Check. Lower right hand corner of the vision board? Also check.

WAS THERE ANY explanation for or connection between the vision board and the watershed time? The skeptic in me was jarred. How was it that these things I'd wished for, even put all kinds of massive effort into, didn't happen until I put them up there, and yet came about because of circumstances beyond my control?

As my friend Amber, a life coach and yoga teacher, put it, "Anyone willing to make a vision board is willing to play outside the realm of black and white. It's a grounded way of playing with magic. You're giving yourself permission to tap into this energy through a game. Energy flows where attention goes. A vision board doesn't make your dreams come true—it's a piece of the puzzle."

A critical piece? Perhaps. Hutson, simultaneously a logical-minded scientist and vision board maker, offered his pragmatic perspective on why it seemed to have worked.

"There are benefits to positive thinking," he said, "even if they aren't truly magical. Research shows that expecting something good to happen can increase self-confidence and help you make it happen. You're also more likely to recognize the opportunities that can lead you to a desired outcome. The trick is that you can't just envision the end result. You have to picture all the steps and obstacles along the way, and how you will get to the end. You need to come up with a plan."

Akin to Niels Bohr with his horseshoe, I still cannot fully believe in vision boards, but that doesn't mean they don't work—whether it's energy flowing where attention's going or something else. "Some of their efficacy is an illusion," Hutson told me, "and to the degree that they do work, it's not through the law of attraction."

Even noted rationalist Barbara Ehrenreich's book *Living With a Wild God* describes a mystical experience that she, as an atheist, would not allow herself to explore for many years. It could be a coincidence, or there could be more to this magic-and-occult stuff than the skeptic in me would allow me to believe.

The uncanny coincidences reinvigorated the idea of a little magic, the unknowable lurking behind what can be concretely perceived. And so I remain a skeptic who entertains herself with possibilities of faith. Eventually I confessed to New Age Kassi about boycotting her original party.

"You said you were out of town!" she said, laughing.

"I was actively *upset* that you were making vision boards."

"As long as it's not hurting anybody, I err on the side of belief," she said.

I lean to the side of doubt, but with one caveat: yes, it's crazy, but it seems that—even though I didn't expect it to—my vision board might have worked anyway.

THE HIDDEN GEM
OF AMERICA

THE WIND BEATS a branch against the bedroom window of my attic apartment, startling me awake. *Just a tree, just the wind.* I burrow under the comforter, clamping my eyes shut and wishing for a speedy return to sleep. *Just the wind.*

The Thurber House in Columbus, Ohio, where I'm spending October as writer-in-residence, is haunted. So the stories—ghost stories—go, so many that the house has been featured on the Syfy show *Ghost Hunters.* The docent told me all about it on the ride from the airport: one night piano keys started playing themselves, leading a former writer-in-residence to become so upset she moved into a hotel for the remainder of her residency. Another heard kitchen cabinets rattling at night.

The rooms on the first two floors of the Victorian mansion are furnished as they were when American humorist James Thurber lived here while attending Ohio State from 1913 to 1917. The house is a living museum, meaning you can touch everything from the old typewriter to the piano keys to the period-style dress displayed on the second floor that's eerie at night, backlit from the streetlamp. I feel like a time traveler when I open the door for Domino's Pizza: *I'm a lady who lives in a museum.*

By day, I work in the office, foliage outside my window turning shades of vibrant red and orange—hues, I imagine, of the fire the night the Ohio Lunatic Asylum, which stood on these grounds, burned down in 1868. The people who died in that fire are the ones said to haunt this place. Forty-seven years later, Thurber's own otherworldly experience inspired his story "The Night the Ghost Got In." I don't believe in ghosts. I put no stock in these stories. Until I am delivered one of my own.

THE MORNING AFTER the windstorm, groggy from lack of sleep, I step out of the bedroom to brew coffee in the kitchenette before settling in at my desk for the day. In the doorway I freeze like a hunted animal. An apple rests in the center of the living room floor, between the couch and coffee table. Baffled, I stare as if still inside a dream, like if I stare long enough, the apple will fade and I'll wake up. But I don't wake up, of course, because I'm already awake.

I'D BROUGHT IN groceries the previous afternoon, entering through the front door of the writers' apartment, where a short hallway leads directly to the kitchenette. There, I unloaded the fruit. There were exactly five apples, which I placed in a bowl on the counter. Now, in the bowl, are four. The living room, where the wayward apple now sits, is far to the right of the mini-kitchen. These already separate spaces are further divided by a huge sectional couch that the 1980s forgot. There is no slope to the carpeted floor. Even if the apple fell, it couldn't have rolled, and even if it rolled, it would have been too large to fit underneath the couch. I can find no sense to make of the bizarre apple migration.

The first person with whom I try to unearth a rational cause is Jason. We have nightly dates on Skype, which ironically feel like a nineteenth-century courtship. Seeing each other but unable to touch: it's the modern-day balcony scene. I feel as if I've traveled back to the era when the Ohio Lunatic Asylum stood here. Every night, my computer chimes at ten because he gets home from capoeira at eight in California. His smile takes up half the screen, and I can't stop staring and grinning myself.

"An animal got in and did it," Jason suggests.

"No bite marks and no evidence of transport." I lower my voice, as if whatever *it* is might hear. "Is there any other explanation than a ghost moved my apple?"

Jason—like me, a skeptic, but without the part that leans toward belief in the unknowable—thinks it's ridiculous to believe in the ghost, but at the Thurber House, no one is surprised.

"It's a playful ghost," a docent says when I show her a photo I took of the apple in the middle of the living room floor. "Don't be afraid."

Still, I barricade myself in the bedroom and stay on Skype with Jason every night until dawn. Fortunately, he doesn't seem to mind. We're dredging up ghosts, too, delving into our past mistakes, humiliations, and relationships. I tell him about having been married twice and the circumstances of each. I tell him about The Fake Trip and The Destruction, and how The Helicopter Pilot propelled me into capoeira. He tells me that he spent close to that number of years with the same person, but never felt certain enough to move toward anything as hopefully permanent as marriage. The distance barrier somehow dissolves the initial awkwardness that tends to go along with early dating, or maybe we just feel particularly at ease in each other's (virtual) company. For someone so opposed to online dating, I'm happy to have these early dates in front of my laptop screen. Not being able to touch or kiss or have sex keeps me in a more levelheaded state of mind.

Except one thing: on an early expedition to the Short North district, I glimpse a wedding dress in the window of a store and think, *I'm going to get married in that dress.*

There's no way I'm getting married anytime soon. Jason is fresh out of a five-year relationship, and given my history I have taken a vow with myself to go slow with new love, to not Half-Danish myself into believing the next intelligent, articulate, handsome guy who comes along is my ideal life partner. I've also promised myself not to have sex before commitment again, because I'm not a person who can successfully disentangle emotions and sex. It sounds as if my mother's advice has gotten through to me after all, at least as far as controlling my romantic impulses with a dose of skepticism rather than going in wholehearted with pure belief.

THOUGH MY TEMPORARY home is haunted, I'm more nervous about Jason's upcoming visit than I am about possibly being pelted by an apple in my sleep. During the third week of my residency, he's coming to Columbus for a four-day-long first "IRL" date. How can we not immediately beeline into my cozy, temporary bedroom given the way our chemistry has been striking even via Skype, and the inevitable fact that a long-distance date must involve a sleepover? When not working or hiding from the ghost, I explore Columbus, pedaling an old bike stored in the basement of the Thurber House down the wide-open sidewalks, thinking about Jason. I hope our long conversations mean more than just the rush of early attraction, but I've been excited about people before and none of them have been right for me. What if I let myself get carried away by potential again, only to again be let down when it doesn't hold up? Is it true that "the best way to find out if you can trust somebody is to trust them"? When I've gone all-in before, it's led to the loss of property and/or dignity. I'm a little bit haunted, too—by the phantoms of past relationships, the kinds that descend from the attic to hover over new ones.

AN ARTICLE IN *Mother Jones* magazine calls Columbus "the new Brooklyn." Before spending a month here I would have believed that like I believed in ghosts. As a myopic New Yorker, I pictured a drive-through city in a flyover state. But I feel a strange and unexpected connection to Columbus, a cool and charming urban wonderland, except with no tourists and no lines. Cities are like people that way—we have an instant and mysterious familiarity with some, even when they are brand-new to us, as if we have known them before. A certain alchemy. I map out all the places I love in the new city I love that I want to show to the man I am loving from afar who will soon arrive, no longer disembodied—ghostly?—on a screen, but in the flesh.

Jason lands in Columbus on a Thursday evening, October 18. My anxiety surges as I wait at Port Columbus Airport. What if our old-fashioned courtship has all been in my mind and it's weird or blasé when we actually see each other? What if he's just rebounding, and I'm a quick fling to get over a long-term relationship that didn't work out?

I spot him in his black hooded sweatshirt and jeans, trademark shaved head and trimmed beard, big dark-brown eyes that felt familiar when I first met him. His charismatic smile spreads as he sees me. I run toward him and take a leap. He drops his carry-on and catches me. He is so handsome, his hug so warm I want to linger in it indefinitely. He tastes of the mint gum I don't yet know he chews perpetually. He smells as if he took a shower and did laundry on the flight over—all soap and dryer sheets. On the drive back to the house, we kiss at every red light.

On arrival, I disarm the security system and give him the official tour memorized from the docents, proud as if this was my own home. Jason agrees that if there were ghosts, they would probably live here. We kick off our everything-backward first date with a bath in the clawfoot tub. We've never seen each other naked and have been clear before the visit that we aren't going to jump into sex just because we happen to be ridiculously attracted to each other and sharing a bed for the next three nights. Though it's tempting, we avoid looking directly at each other as we disrobe and enter the bubble bath, all the while chatting and making plans for the long weekend ahead as if we're some old couple that's known each other for decades. When we get out and dry off, we still haven't seen each other naked. Not an easy feat, but I am sticking to my resolution, and the chaste bath is somehow even sexier anyway.

Post-bath and pre-date, Jason asks, "So . . . will you be my girl-friend?"—as in, skip the whole dating part and go straight to commit-ment. I haven't been asked to be somebody's girlfriend since high school. It's a strange question to hear in your thirties, and an impulsive question from a man I'll only later learn is far from an impulsive person. I ques-tion if, having recently gotten out of a long-term relationship, he's look-ing for a replacement, even subconsciously. Yet even though I feel like a proverbial lunatic—a love-lunatic, inhabiting the former grounds of an asylum—I agree. It just feels natural, part of the flow. Our first official date is off to a surreal start given that we're already in a committed relationship before it even begins. If, as living in the Thurber House makes me feel, I've been transported here from another era, I've met a fellow traveler.

The restaurant's decor consists of little pieces of paper mounted by clothespins on string throughout the room, bearing haiku customers have written. We add our own before we go, a small, impermanent marker of our presence, a token of the date left behind. When we have sex for the first time later that night, it's both sex on our first date and not breaking my vow of waiting for a committed relationship.

The next day when I wake up, I wonder if there will be "first morning after" uncomfortable feelings, but the man beside me still feels strangely familiar. After making scrambled eggs and coffee, we take our new relationship out for a walk to the Topiary Garden, which I stumbled on by accident early in my Columbus stay. The land was once a campus for the Deaf School in the early nineteenth century, and now serves as a three-dimensional bushes-and-trees installation of a re-creation of Georges Seurat's Post-Impressionist painting *A Sunday Afternoon on the Island of La Grande Jatte*. We play at the park, making imaginary conversation for the tree sculpture people, hiding from each other behind them. For lunch we have what we agree are the best hot dog (him) and veggie dog (me) either of us has ever eaten, along with a heaping pile of tater tots. Even our food is childlike, and I wonder if a marker of real love is a certain innocence and delight in simplicity. When we pass by the storefront with the wedding dress, I remain silent.

We drive two hours to Amish Country, and he helps me with some acrobatic capoeira moves on the nation's second-largest covered bridge, the Bridge of Dreams. We take silly photos in front of Big Ben, the "Largest Horse in Holmes County," and buy pickled okra at a marketplace. We stroll arm in arm, watching Amish buggies roll by, relics of a simpler way. Back in the city we spend hours in the German Village, walking in Schiller Park and the Book Loft, a bookstore with thirty-two rooms. Jason buys a children's book about a fish with a hat for his classroom. I get a new copy of my favorite by Anne Lamott that had met its fate in a Brooklyn bathtub two years earlier. Nightfall brings us to a dueling piano bar where one performer's improvised version of "Thrift Shop," we agree, is "off the chain," way better than the actual version. Forget Paris. The world's most romantic city is Columbus, Ohio. I'm falling unexpectedly in love in a place I hadn't expected to love. At night in the house, as if aware it must not disturb this universe, the ghost hibernates.

The finale of our unconventional first date is Sunday afternoon at the Annie Leibovitz exhibit at the Wexner Center, a "research laboratory" for the arts on Ohio State's campus. I stand before a photograph of my forever-ideal couple Joan Didion and John Gregory Dunne, reading about the image on my phone, when the guard interrupts.

"That's a violation of the rules," she says. "I'm going to have to ask you to leave."

She thinks I'm taking photographs, which according to posted signage is strictly forbidden. Jason jumps in.

"We're not taking pictures, we're reading about the pictures." He takes my phone and shows it to the guard, the page open to a Wikipedia entry. The guard half-listens to Jason's plea.

"You two are such a cute couple," she interrupts. "All right. No more photographs."

The guard walks away. Jason fumes about the injustice of the accusation ("I did not break a rule," he says). I'm thrilled by her compliment.

We voluntarily depart, wandering through the green campus in the late-afternoon sun, slants of light through the trees. The way this place makes me feel and the way this person makes me feel are enmeshed, and it is indeed alchemical.

Columbus is surprisingly magical. But the new Brooklyn it is not. Places, like relationships, must be appreciated on their own unique terms. Columbus, The Hidden Gem of America. I'm nostalgic for my time here before I've even left. In three weeks, I'll arrive in Jason's home of Santa Cruz the night before my thirty-third birthday. Am I right this time? Am I crazy? What if I'm imagining all this? What if he doesn't really feel the same? Alone again, my fears about making another wrong decision and getting my heart broken haunt me. My paranoid mind worries, *What if he asked me to be his girlfriend because he knew that was the only way I'd sleep with him? And now, having taken that important step toward getting over his ex, he ghosts me?* It would be easy given our homes on opposite coasts. He wouldn't have to explain or have an excuse—the distance could simply be "too much."

I stroll through the Short North, pausing at the window of that wedding dress shop. I've never been interested in wedding dresses. I didn't care what I wore. It was emotional security I was after, back when I thought marriage was sure to deliver as much. But now, for some reason, just when I'm not hoping or planning to get married, the billowy white dress—ghostly in the storefront window—captures my imagination. I'm now reminded of the advice from the by-referral-only tarot reader to my mother, delivered in the form of a reference to Tennessee Williams's play *The Rose Tattoo*: "A girl is going off with a sailor, and he says, 'Is this your first time?' And she says, 'Every time is my first time.' Now, let's say if, the week before, she'd been beaten up by a sailor, she might look at the young sailor and go, *Oh my god, another sailor*. But she's not. This is a whole new sailor."

The Thurber House docent is right. There's no reason to be afraid, not of otherworldly apple drops or the hauntings of past-tense romance. Like new love, ghosts can be playful. They are what you let them be.

33

O N MY THIRTY-THIRD birthday I got engaged for the third time.

THE DAY I was to leave Ohio, Hurricane Sandy slammed into New York. Every flight was cancelled, so I flew west instead. My second date with Jason came sooner than planned. He came up with the "six-month rule": he had to wait six months before proposing, the shortest span of time after which engagement sounded remotely reasonable. "Six months is good," I said. "So is five minutes or ten years. It's all good."

When I found someone I wanted to marry and who seemed to want to marry me, marriage was no longer of the utmost importance. I also knew patience in a way I hadn't before. Marriage wasn't at the forefront of my mind. That we had found each other at all and had made significant changes in a short time to be together—just the way we were—was enough. We knew. I didn't need any validation or input. It was just right.

The hurricane passed, the city devastated in its wake. I returned for a few days. My apartment was unaffected; a friend flooded out of Coney Island had moved in while I was gone. I packed a few suitcases and Baxter and returned to Jason on November 11, Veterans Day, which that year fell on a Sunday, meaning schools were closed on Monday, my birthday. Jason, a teacher, had the day off.

"WHAT DO YOU want to do to celebrate?" he asked when we got up in the morning. There was no question. If Jason had lived in the middle of nowhere in a box I would have gone there. But that he lived here added to his appeal because Monterey Bay is stocked with otters. Santa Cruz's spirit sister cities might be the likes of Boulder, Sedona, and Woodstock, but only Santa Cruz offers the chance to see my spirit animal within hugging range.

"Kayak to see the otters," I said.

I love otters so much I cry when I see them. I thought my emotional reaction upon encountering my furry aquatic soul mates was insane or at least socially inappropriate until I watched actress Kristen Bell have a sloth-meltdown on *Ellen* (YouTube this if you haven't seen it) and felt much better about my w*otter*works (sorry). Kayaking to see otters up close, though, would be the ultimate test of whether Jason could love me when he witnessed my quirks. He didn't seem fazed at the prospect, but he hadn't seen it.

My heart palpitated as Jason called the kayak rental to make a reservation. This was going to be the best birthday ever.

Then it wasn't.

The kayak rental was closed.

"Oh no," he said, more disappointed than I was. "I failed to produce otters on your birthday!"

He was genuinely sorry. I didn't mind, I assured him. The otters weren't jumping ship from their kelp beds. This wasn't an early-date fail like showing up drunk spilling flowers while dressed as a certain other kind of aquatic animal. We lay on the bed talking about what we would do instead (Redwoods hike? Cliff walk? Movie?), but soon trailed off into other subjects and sex, and suddenly it was already late afternoon and we hadn't left the apartment. It could have ended with that and still been the best birthday I'd ever had.

Then Jason threw his six-month rule out the window.

"Want to get married?" he said. "Will you marry me?"

I studied his face to see if he was serious. He was. It was a huge surprise, but following my instincts and my "profiling," there was no question I would say yes.

Jason and I had something to do instead of look for otters: look for rings. It was already past four in the afternoon. The stores would be closing soon. We hurried to a jewelry store on Pacific Street, the main stretch of downtown around the corner from his studio, a street with no traffic lights. Unlike New York, the city that never sleeps, Santa Cruz sleeps all the time. If it were any more laid-back it wouldn't have a pulse. There weren't any appealing rings in that first shop, but the woman behind the counter told us to try a place called Judi Wyant Antiques, down the other end of Pacific, which offered more selection. It was closing in five minutes, so we ran and got there just in time for me to try on a bunch of rings, really fast. I found the one, a vintage 1920s ring that's pretty but understated, right away, but proceeded to try on more just to be sure. It turned out, of course, that the one is the one.

Though it was my third engagement, it was also my first proposal. I'd proposed to Emir, and Julian had slipped a ring on my finger while I slept—twice.

After my struggles, bad decisions, hesitations, and doubts, when it happened it happened smoothly and easily. Instead of visiting Santa Cruz for three weeks and seeing how it went from there, I was making an unexpected move. Jason did offer to move to Brooklyn, if that was what I wanted. But what I wanted was to join him in this zephyrean beachside paradise, where sea lion barks under the pier replaced subway rumblings beneath sidewalk grates. Where drivers stop if they see a pedestrian so much as eyeball a crosswalk.

MY FRIEND (THE good ex) Andy ascribed special significance to thirty-three as a number-slash-age that holds some kind of magic. It was a sign, when he saw it along his path, that he was headed in the right direction. He had a Facebook page for it and everything. I thought this was another one of the many eccentric traits that added up to Andy, but I read an interview with Katy Perry in *Elle* magazine where she too speaks of the power of thirty-three. There's no real explanation for this, of course, only a string of coincidences (for those interested, Wikipedia lists them all), but that seems to be what it takes to believe there's more to something beneath its surface. I could see the reasons for believing in certain occult practices (tarot, vision boards), but numerology was too esoteric even for me. Then someone said, "You will have been married three times by thirty-three. That seems like something." Is it? Is thirty-three a "magic" number? I don't know if I believe that, but it was a year when years of magical thinking paid off.

THE PROFILER WAS not so easily convinced. She worried that I was doing another rash thing—which I was, but her concern was that its rashness implied another mistake. She wanted to screen them out quickly, but when I met the right one at warp speed, it was suspect. (I can give her credit for that. It is, after all, the fact of the matter. I'd later find out New Age Kassi had been particularly worried. "You just disappeared to California. I was waiting for it to blow up, and expecting you to show back up in New York.")

"The Profiler says no!" my mother said when I told her I was moving. "I'm going to write about it on the blog!"

"Oh no you're not," I said, immediately protective of Jason.

And anyway, she'd approved him, in a roundabout way, even if she wouldn't admit to it. My mother had been visiting during batizado week, the week following my vision board party. She met Jason when he was in my apartment at a capoeira-people brunch. Later, when I asked her, as The Profiler, her opinion of my capoeira guy friends, she singled him out.

"Jason is interesting. He made an effort to come over and talk to me. He's charismatic and bright."

Without any of us knowing it at the time, Jason passed the Profiler test. At my dining table the morning he met her, I'd showed Jason the "When Mom Is on the Scent" article that had been published the day we left the Ithaca retreat. He read it on the spot, laughing at certain parts. "Hilarious and totally ridiculous," he said.

And after everything, I did profile Jason. I noted his employment status: six years in his current job, known in his district as "the behavior guy," solving the problems of children with special needs on a daily basis. Passions for things outside of work: capoeira instructor, politics, history aficionado, writing, hiking. Friendships: many. Alcohol consumption:

sparing. Drugs: none. Eating and cooking habits: lots of vegetables, likes to cook. Sexual hang-ups: none. Depressive or manic tendencies: none. Even his sleeping habits (deep-sleeping night owls, both of us) were on target. It made sense on paper, without sacrificing physical chemistry. Though I'd been similarly interested in Half-Danish and The Diplomat, it wasn't mutual, and I now was glad. Whereas I was trying to force something to happen in those cases, Jason was right for me. No forcing.

As a special education teacher, Jason was also great at communicating effectively with The Profiler. He helped me strategize how to do so, too, with his extensive training in behavior modification.[9]

With The Profiler protesting, I resolved to keep Jason from her screening tactics.

"You're being defensive because you know I'm right," she said.

She was. It was all happening so fast. I was giving up my home and life in New York to move to Santa Cruz and be with Jason. It looked as if I was repeating impulsive past behavior, doing something rash. Yet I had to, and that was the part I couldn't explain to my mother or anyone because, again, love is not a rational force. I had to take a risk, not ask The Profiler or the tarot reader or anyone if it was okay. I'd let The Profiler in, given her a fair chance to test her skill on my love life after years of resistance. And this was where it had led.

My mother and I fell right back into our old roles; she worried and implored me to heed her warnings lest I make a mistake; I withdrew and became withholding. Though this time, I could understand. She'd done the same thing with my father that I was about to do with Jason, married after knowing each other for three months, and it hadn't worked out as she'd wanted. Still, as she always said, she doesn't have regrets because she has me. There's no predicting an outcome, but she inadvertently helped prove my original point: a relationship that doesn't work out isn't a waste.

---

9 See Appendix B: The Special Ed Behavior Modification Expert's Manual for Getting Controlling Mothers Under Control.

When I met Jason's parents at an Italian restaurant the weekend after he proposed, Jason's mother had a different take: "You're both in your thirties. You have enough life experience by now to know what's right when you find it. It doesn't take as long." She's a great foil for The Profiler, though she was essentially saying the same thing differently framed—that through trial and error over time, we know enough to become our own profilers. To trust intuition. We can only rely on our best instincts in the present moment to guide us. Like my mother's, my gut reactions had often been right, even—especially—ones I'd chosen to ignore.

As The Profiler's daughter, I'd become, with our experiment, finally attuned to my own inclinations.

Over the holidays, Jason and I went to Mexico, a trip that involved both romance and food poisoning. At two months together, that I wanted him to be the one holding back my hair as I vomited all night was a great sign. When he vomited pink Pedialyte on the bus the next morning, I couldn't hold back his hair—Jason doesn't have hair to hold back—but reached out my empty iced-drink Starbucks cup just in time to prevent him from throwing up on the floor of the bus.

"Looks like a strawberry Frappuccino," we agreed.

Amusement, indeed.

WHEN JASON RETURNED from work in the afternoons of our early days living together in Santa Cruz, we took a lot of walks downtown to the boba tea shop or farmers market. It felt as if we were on our earliest dates, which we were, yet we were also already engaged. What if I discovered some big ugly secret yet to be revealed because we hadn't known each other very long? Fortunately, even habits that might have irritated other people were compatible. Jason immerses himself in articles on BBC News and Slate, multiple times a day. Sometimes for a really long time. It's as if he enters a portal to another world via his phone. Then he engages in political debates on Facebook, because somewhere on the internet, someone is wrong.

Still, I rarely ask him to put the phone down because I'm ultimately glad for his encyclopedic knowledge of current events, politics, and history. I can ask him about a candidate or issue and hear all the information nicely synthesized by his sponge-brain. So the very thing that annoys me is also something I wouldn't want to change. The activity that disconnects him from me also makes for lively discussions when he comes back from phone-land.

I did eventually discover Jason's big ugly secret. We have differing relationships to the ocean. When I was moving to Santa Cruz, I envisioned taking up surfing. Assuming Jason surfed because he lived in one of the surfing capitals of the nation, I thought he could help me learn to catch waves at Cowells, the go-to beginner spot.

"I hate surfing," Jason said. "Catching a wave is not worth all that time sitting and waiting in the boring-ass ocean."

He said it with a smile.

"Boring? You can see seals, feel the sun on your face. You can daydream."

Jason, still smiling through my speech, found my Profiler-esque efforts to convince him charming, but he could not be convinced. I found out I like the way he digs in his heels when he has strong feelings about something. I eventually acquiesced, and also learned I most enjoy surfing solitary.

"WAS THERE EVER a moment you had doubts about me or worried you were making a terrible mistake?" I ask four years later in our living room. Jason is about to take Baxter on her afternoon walk. He's come back in for his wallet so he can go to the bookstore to get the *Game of Thrones* prequel stories. He pauses, thinking for a moment. Baxter tilts her head in the particular gesture of pug-listening.

"When I first showed up in Ohio I worried for a second right before I saw you," he says. "What if I came all the way out here and we had an awkward friend-y thing going on—what if I totally misinterpreted all the signals? And the first time we had a fight . . . well it wasn't a fight, it was a 'grump.' You were mad at me about my not rushing to clean the house, and I thought, *Oh no, what if it's been all best-case scenario and this is what she's really like? What if she always gets mad at me at the drop of a hat for no reason and then is passive-aggressive all day?*"

"Uh-huh. And how did these concerns resolve?"

"When I got to Ohio the first thing you did was jump on me and give me a kiss, so that solves that. And your 'grump' went away, and we made up. But yeah, the first time we got in a fight we were already engaged, and I thought, *What if she hasn't been acting like her normal self the whole time?* We just had a basic communication error, but I thought for a second, *What if this is her regular way of being and she's been hiding it?* But we talked about it and everything was fine."

"So how did you know I was the one for you?"

"I don't know . . ." he says, "I could talk with you all day and never get bored, you're kooky and weird in the same way I'm kooky and weird. Our kooky weirdnesses fit together like puzzle pieces."

"Aww. Okay, this helps. Thanks. Bye."

"Bye!" he disappears out the door to go buy *A Knight of the Seven Kingdoms.*

WE FOUND A place to get married in the Santa Cruz Mountains, a place we nicknamed the Buddhist Resort for its Tibetan prayer flags strung around the property. I told Jason about the dress I'd seen in Columbus. He didn't freak out that a wedding dress had caught my eye before our first date. He thought it was a great idea to return for another Columbus long-weekend date to commemorate our everlasting love and oh yeah get that dress.

"You've already been married," The Profiler said in horror. "I don't think you're supposed to wear white!"

"I'm pretty sure there's no longer anything you're 'supposed to' wear or not," I said. "Anyway, it's my first wedding to the right guy, so I want to do it right this time, too."

"Right" meant that dress, which was, like the marriage I was about to enter, traditional yet modern.

EVERY COUPLE HAS their special place. Columbus would be ours. In February, Jason and I returned for a long weekend. We stayed in the Thurber House's attic apartment. It was the off-season for the writers-in-residence program, and the director thought it was romantic that we were coming back to the site of our long-weekend first date to get my wedding dress.

We brought along paper invitations to snail-mail to older relatives. When I emerged from the bedroom the first morning in the Thurber House apartment, the invitations were scattered on the floor around the table. The ghost!

"See?" I said. "There aren't any windows open. How do you explain this?"

"Things fall all the time," Jason said. "There could be a draft or something. There's not a ghost."

"There isn't a draft," I argued.

I left the invitations on the little table in the apartment, and we went back to the Short North for the dress in the window. Then we returned to the Bridge of Dreams for a two-person commitment ceremony of our own. Jason surprised me with matching *Legend of Zelda* triforce rings. On the inside one read, "It's Dangerous . . ." and the other, ". . . To Go Alone." (We both like Zelda.)

When we walked back into the apartment, the wedding invitations were arranged in a neat little path toward the fire door, in a way that could not have been random. My chest felt crushed, as if I'd had the wind knocked out of me. I was suddenly freezing. A scream I didn't recognize as my own voice left my body. Tears rushed to my eyes.

"Oh my god, did you do this? Please tell me you did this."

I was hyperventilating by then, and Jason would later say he was planning to mess with me a little more until he saw how upset I was.

"Yeeessssss . . ."

"How could you?"

By then the tears I was wiping were from laughter. It all shifted in an instant. We were both cracking up.

IN AUGUST OF 2013, Jason proceeded down the aisle in a redwood grove to the dulcet tones of the *Legend of Zelda* symphony. Emir walked me to the altar for the third and final time. A capoeira roda broke out at the reception. And The Profiler gave a memorable speech.

"She doesn't tell her mother anything," she said. "The next thing I know, I'm fired from being The Profiler, she doesn't want me to do that anymore, and she's moving all the way to California for this Jason . . . and the mother doesn't know what's going on, Lize doesn't tell me anything, but here we are today . . . so, a toast to Liza and Jason. Cin cin! Saluti! L'chaim!"

Some things don't change—for better or for worse.

And yet, years later, my mother would send this advice in response to an email chain request for New Year's inspirational quotes: "Don't let the noise of others' opinions drown out your own inner voice. And most important, have the courage to follow your heart and intuition." I had learned much from her. Had she learned something from me?

SARA ECKEL, AUTHOR of *It's Not You*, says on the subject of finding the right one after years of failed dating and relationships: "We didn't have a major growth experience, we just met a guy." I, though, did need to experience growth before I was ready to find Jason. The Profiler journey didn't find me a husband—or it did, indirectly, depending on how you look at it—but it taught me some things I needed to know. It's not that there aren't complications when it's right, but rather that when it's right, the complications are uncomplicated. They fall away. When it's right, you don't need The Profiler or anyone to tell you. You just know, and your person will know the same about you, and you will be that person's French Girl, glaringly and without a doubt.

I also learned that what I really needed was an arranged marriage.

Jason and I say this as a joke, but the primary quality that continues to surprise me four years into our togetherness is that we're in an arranged marriage, arranged by us.

Everything was backward: Falling in love over Skype. Already in love by our first date, which required air travel. Committed before our first date yet also sex on our first date—simultaneously hitting and breaking rules I'd made after my previous relationships (no sex prior to commitment, no sex on a first date). Got engaged on our third date, then moved in together. In our fourth month, bought a house. Took a honeymoon to Brazil. Got married on return. Total = eight months.

It was The Profiler's nightmare and also what she'd been asking for all along: to know quickly. It works. Though now, three years married with a baby on the way, Jason and I are still in the honeymoon stage of dating.

A note from the desk of

THE PROFILER

THE PROFILER WAS in shock when Liza met Jason and precipitously moved her dog, suitcases, and books cross-country to be with him. From New York City to Santa Cruz. What was she thinking?

When I met Jason in Brooklyn at my daughter's apartment at a capoeira group party, The Profiler's first reaction was positive. Self-confident, with a firm handshake and friendly smile, he came over to talk to me. A special education teacher with an apartment in Santa Cruz. *Nice friend for Liza*, I thought. Then abruptly, the scenario dramatically changed. As Jason suddenly morphed from capoeira friend to romantic interest, The Profiler's anxiety surged. Bicoastal dating? Wasn't there a future husband for her already settled and working in New York? Rushing across the U.S. for someone she didn't really know? Impulsive and thoughtless?

Heart over mind, again, The Profiler would say. Take a breath—time for some analytical thinking. Mostly Liza followed her heart, though she insists that she "profiled Jason, too." Fortunately, this time her instincts were on target and she found a great match. Positive qualities she sought (intelligent, supportive, honest, kind with a sense of humor, and with common interests), plus a strong dose of the magic "spark."

Years of profiling my daughter's dates were over. From surreptitiously glimpsing some on Facebook, to meeting others in person; from seeking "potential mates" on my blog, to finally seeing who the real Mr. Right would turn out to be: years of experiences and conversations about romance, love, and how to know if a guy is really the one for you.

Looking for love is a common denominator of human existence. Where is my "soul mate"? Is it him/her? How will I know for sure? Hopefully, profiling will help! Try it and let me know.

THE MANIFESTATION
OF SEÑOR BACON

JASON AND I first talked about adopting a potbelly pig pet during one of our nightly Skype conversations, succumbing to the internet-age pastime of browsing cute animal photos. Together, on our respective screens, we looked at pig pictures. I joked about getting one of our own.

"We could name him Señor Bacon," Jason said.

"I hope you know you just made this a real thing," I said.

Still, Jason was kidding, and I figured I probably was, too. But after moving in together, Jason and I started playing a game in which Señor Bacon began making ghostly appearances. "I saw his little hoof prints outside today," Jason would say. Señor Bacon's "disembodied pig spirit" left us surprise gifts: a cheesy straw giraffe or llama—we called it the llamaraffe—I'd pretended to admire at a furniture store, and several pairs of Jason's favorite kind of socks, stuffed into his drawer to be discovered. Señor Bacon Day replaced Christmas—he was the one who delivered presents in the night. Jason and I relished quirky forms of amusement. Though he was the one I'd been looking for, for years, without knowing what exactly I was seeking, what I definitely hadn't known was that I'd also end up seeking a potbelly piglet. "Just for fun," we told ourselves, as we looked into pig breeders online, but they were far away in rural Missouri or Oklahoma. And what would we be getting into with this whole pig thing anyway? Would taking our fictional pig into the realm of reality be disastrous? We knew there was no such thing as a mini-pig. He could very well grow to five hundred pounds. Where would we put him? I could never take in an animal and then get rid of him. If we did go through with Señor Bacon, we would be entering a commitment that, like caring for a young child, would last over a decade.

But after living with the fantasy gift-giving pig for months, the desire to get the real one grew. It had become an eight-month-long running joke, though, and I'd begun to doubt we were ever really going to get him. We'd probably have a family first—kids, something that we also both agreed we wanted but that still felt abstract.

One Saturday, we took the pug to the dog beach. As we approached the steps leading down to the sand, I did a double-take: there was a woman walking a pig on a leash.

Señor Bacon must be on my mind, because now I'm hallucinating pigs. That has to be a dog. We reached the top of the staircase at the same time. I wasn't delusional. Walking on the leash beside the woman was, indeed, a potbelly pig. It was a coincidence too large to ignore. As I petted the pig, whose bristly fur was gray, pink, and white, I bombarded her with questions.

Her pig, Oblio, was six months old and the same size as Baxter, who sniffed him curiously. Oblio was learning to walk down stairs. He knew some tricks, like "spin around." As Oblio rooted sweetly in the sand, Señor Bacon became more tangible. Our harbinger-of-pig gave me the phone number for a farmer in Fresno—two hours away—who bred small potbellies. I hesitated for three more weeks, then called Farmer Wayne.

The number was disconnected.

I used the online sleuthing skills gained in too many hours stalking exes to sift through pages of unrelated information, but deep into the search, the magic of the internet yielded a LinkedIn profile for Farmer Wayne in Fresno. His profile picture was a pig. I sent a message. Within days, Wayne replied and introduced us to his colleague Tyler, who lived forty-five minutes away. Señor Bacon was even closer than we thought! Tyler had a new batch of piglets, three months old.

When Tyler brought the piglets to town so we could meet them, Jason and I were at a friend's barbecue. Three little piglets showed up in a box at a barbecue. We took turns holding them. As I held the first piglet, he screeched, sounding as if he was being slaughtered rather than cradled. But I knew, even before examining the others. Like his relative Oblio, he was gray and white with pink stripes on either side of his snout. He was tiny, fuzzy, and adorable. Even though he was screaming his head off, I had a feeling he was the one.

"Is this Señor Bacon?" Jason asked.

"I think so, yes."

I don't know how I knew. It was just a feeling. The piglet was still shrieking. I put him back into the box. Pigs don't like being picked up. Because they are prey animals, when their hooves leave the ground it triggers the sensation that they are about to enter the jaws of a carnivorous beast. "You can train him out of it," Tyler said.

When Jason came home with Señor a few days later, we had a bed, a baby gate, toys, food, and water waiting in his area (the laundry room). We had literally brought home the Bacon. It was amazing and terrifying. The way I had imagined meeting one's baby for the first time was: *Well, he's here, now what?* Unlike an infant, though, Señor did not desire any physical closeness. He hid in his bed under blankets, emerging to eat and drink before going back into hiding. The reality of owning a pig was much different from the imaginary pig spirit who left us presents.

"He doesn't seem to like us," I said.

"He's just not used to us yet," Jason said.

What if he never warmed to us? He was little and scared, and I was a little bit scared of him. I wasn't sure how to interact. He was indifferent to all the stuffed animals and toys and didn't like being touched. I worried we'd made a mistake. What if Señor Bacon was better off left as the imaginary pig? The idea vs. the reality: the same feeling that made me nervous when I thought about having a kid. We needed some guidance.

Jason and I joined potbelly pig groups on Facebook. Thousands of members passionate about their pigs were gold mines of advice. They lived on farms and in apartments across the nation and internationally. I found myself spending hours admiring tiny spotted Albert from the

U.K., big Cletus of Kentucky, and Hobey, who was briefly famous for being kicked off a US Airways flight.

Soon Señor Bacon had a ball pit to root around in for carrots and lettuce, a puzzle game, and his own cashmere blanket. We got him a harness made especially for pig bodies and took him for short walks downtown. As we finally figured out how to care for him, he slowly began to trust us. He made occasional small displays of affection—nosing at our feet or rolling over for a tummy rub. We learned that a pig's love must be won. I bought a manual called *Potbellied Pig Parenting*.

Señor Bacon eventually learned he could trust us and warmed up to his adoptive parents. He ate carrots from my hand and woke us at five in the morning, singing out of tune for his breakfast. He taught himself to jump up on the couch, rooting on pillows and surprising me by snuggling up in my lap. He was getting closer to our initial imaginary friend version of him, though he's still grouchy, obstinate, and stubborn.

When I cook dinner, Señor Bacon enters the kitchen expectantly, emitting his vacuum cleaner grumbles, looking up at me with his brown eyes, eager for a bite of the vegetables I'm stirring. He is nature's composting solution, eating every kind of fruit and vegetable scrap except bell pepper tops, onions, and basil. During housebreaking, I gave him celery, carrots, zucchini, and his favorite, strawberries, for doing his business outside. Potty training: check. But this, too, is a nonlinear process.

One of the Great Lakes began to form on our kitchen floor. That pigs are prolific urinators is one of the many things I did not yet know in those days before Señor Bacon morphed from pig spirit to actual pig—with a bladder large enough to produce Lake Eerie. I ushered him outside, where he promptly resumed digging trenches in the yard with his nose. It took months to correct our miscommunication (urinating = treats!), but he finally got it, trotting out to the deck on his own to relieve himself.

SEÑOR BACON MAKES his short walks long, stopping to root, chomp acorns, and devour clover by the bushel on the way. He tends to draw a crowd. At night, he hops up on the couch to wedge into a lap or an armpit. He has ditched his own bed in favor of ours. One night, Señor Bacon took a flying leap up into the bed, tucking his hooves under while trying to shove us over with his snout. At first, I protested. Yes, Baxter slept there, but a pig in the bed was just strange. Jason alluded to Señor Bacon's potential as a foot-warmer on chilly winter nights. As he buried under the blankets and we rested our feet against his little body, the coziness was indeed convincing. Eventually, though, he does get moved back to the laundry room after he destroys a comforter by climbing into bed after being sprayed by a skunk.

Pigs are perpetual toddlers. We have had to babyproof the house—Señor Bacon opens drawers and kitchen cabinets, shredding paper plates and napkins, scattering objects around, leaving a trail of chaos in his wake. He throws tantrums when he wants attention or treats, doing his pterodactyl screech. I realize we have inadvertently trained ourselves for having kids. Though it's impending, childbearing has still remained ethereal in my plan because my lack of experience with babies makes me nervous about having one. I don't actually know any babies, not in close proximity—some friends' kids, but I see them from a distance, the same way I pass by otters while kayaking. They're adorable, but kept at arm's length because they may bite if you get too close.

Señor Bacon changed this. With this new confidence in my ability to love and care for a loud, messy, obnoxious, moody, and destructive little creature, I am ready to stop not-trying to have a baby. I have learned how to deal with tantrums, pee on the floor, and keeping anything I don't want destroyed on a high shelf.

A year to the date of the pig's arrival, I learn I am pregnant.

During my pregnancy, Señor Bacon can't nose me on the couch as usual. He might root too hard on my protruding belly or, worse, step on it with his sharp and pointy hooves. As distance grows between us, there are even times when I admit to myself that life would be easier if we didn't have him.

"Why *do* you have that pig?" my mother asks. "I don't like him."

"Let me guess . . . he's not 'right for me'?"

But the unruly pig has been a huge part (at fifty pounds) of our happy domestic chaos. My mother doesn't approve of Señor Bacon, but I do. He wouldn't fit into her life, but he fits into Jason's and mine. At least most of the time. He's grumpy. He monopolizes Jason's lap space. He growls and bites our guests. Looking back at a self-help book I bought in the wake of a past separation called *Why Does He Do That? Inside the Minds of Angry and Controlling Men*, I can see that Señor Bacon matches the profile of The Demand Man. Some relationships need work, and some—for instance, this one—are worth putting in that effort. I pause in a sunlit spot on the deck to pet his snout. "Don't worry, buddy," I tell him. "You'll always be Mamma's first little terror."

A few months later, Jason and I are on the couch binge-watching comedian Aziz Ansari's Netflix show *Master of None*. When Ansari's protagonist takes his soon-to-be girlfriend Rachel on an early date to Nashville, we agree that weekend-long travel dating is actually a great way to find out if someone is right for you—are your travel styles compatible? Sounds like something out of The Profiler's playbook. But we have to rewind and play it again when the characters, too, have a flirtatious conversation about getting a potbelly pig. Now that Jason and I have actually owned our demon pterodactyl for awhile, I'd tell them it's probably a lot like having children: way more romantic in theory, and also totally worth it.

STARS BURNED
TWICE AS BRIGHT

A YEAR AFTER ANDY and I broke up, he bought a van and drove across the country to go to Burning Man and make a documentary. As his world was expanding exponentially, mine was contracting, womblike, into the domestic existence I'd longed for and feared impossible.

IN MY LAID-BACK, small-city routine, I obsessively watched the very different journey Andy chronicled online. He'd racked up thousands of followers. A flicker of excitement registered every time my Notifications showed a new Andy post. He got his van stuck in the mud. He wore a furry vest with nothing underneath in the middle of Times Square. He helped the homeless in Reno in a pirate costume. He stood on top of his van wearing a unicorn head. Andy hadn't been right for me, but he was right for so many other people, just as he'd said when I accused him of spouting hippie nonsense. So many Facebook posts from so many people told stories of how Andy had changed their perspective, or their lives.

Though I was glad he was pursuing his whimsy, I also had a Profiler-like concern: for someone who had spent his life up until then being rational and responsible, how had he gone so far, and so fast? "This is how people become homeless," a mutual friend said on glimpsing one of Andy's photos in his newsfeed.

"Burnt . . . just charred stars at this point," another wrote on a photo Andy had posted of a sunrise after staying up all night.

Andy's unconventional choices made him an easy target. He knew it, too, but countered any sarcasm with his trademark sincerity. "But still burning BRIGHT. It's a new life . . . and I'm feeling good."

I observed Andy's new life in a state of bewildered curiosity. He drove around the United States, making new friends and reconnecting with old ones, posting about driving through the night and his incredible lack of need for virtually any sleep. I was happy he was finding value on his vision quest but at the same time worried all his sparkle was a reaction to some deep pain.

"You live so hard," somebody commented.

"Making up for lost time," he responded.

ON ONE OF his brief West Coast stops after Burning Man in early September of 2013, the month after Jason and I got married, Andy dropped by to visit. He'd turned into Andy-plus: more theatrical, wearing whirling dervish costumes as everyday clothes. He told even longer stories. I took him to the pier to see the sea lions while he told me about falling in love with a mermaid at Burning Man. He walked around downtown in a silver burqa, only his eyes peering out from behind the sparkling fabric. *Thankfully it's Santa Cruz right after Burning Man, or this might be intolerably strange*, I thought. I smiled and went along with it.

I asked how the documentary was going.

"I'm working on it. But it's only a small part of what I've learned this journey is. The real art is my life."

He'd received an inheritance, and with budgetary time constraints removed, the movie was unfolding into a larger, more personal story that transcended being just a project. "I'm a professional appreciator of moments," he said.

And then he was standing in my kitchen, meeting my husband. As I made us salads, Andy told Jason the mermaid story.

"A woman who was dressed as a mermaid?" Jason asked.

"No," Andy said. "*A mermaid.*"

Andy's so dramatic and fun, I thought. It never would have worked between us. Spending an hour with both of them in the same room concretized as much, displaying the stark contrast between my rooted life with Jason and the rambling one Andy created for himself. But I loved counting Andy as a friend. He was the one ex-boyfriend who could transition into platonic territory. His journey showed me how much your choice of partner creates and impacts your daily existence. I could have lived in a world where mermaids were real, and everyone was on a cosmic quest toward some ultimate magical destiny, where I would have been a passenger on a Ken Kesey–esque acid bus to Burning Man, searching for those "secrets of the universe." ("Secret of the Universe: If you are in a place and you are not feeling it for whatever reason, GO WANDER, and the universe will put you exactly where you are supposed to be.")

Had things gone differently, I might have been on board, but I had moved away from that path, the one that became the path of Andy. It was a good road—for him. And it made me understand exactly how much I needed the family photos lining the shelf above the fireplace, and the extent to which I needed to follow Flaubert's advice to "be steady and well-ordered in your life, so that you may be violent and original in your work."

I wouldn't call my life with Jason regular or ordinary. However, we were the kind of happy family that would make a poor dead Russian novelist roll over in his grave. I like to think we're happy in our own unique way—snuggling Señor Bacon on the couch at night, attending Brazilian Fight Club . . . nah, who am I kidding—I became regular. I became boring! And I'd never been happier.

I walked Andy out to his van that day to say goodbye.

"Are you sure you don't want to stay for dinner?" I asked.

He opened the passenger door and pointed to a Crock-Pot connected to the lighter portal. He lifted the lid, revealing a steaming chicken stew.

"Nope, got dinner going right here."

This was both innovative and troubling. I felt my old patterns firing up, but Andy was a friend, and I didn't treat my friends as home-repair projects. It wasn't my responsibility to help him, and he didn't need help. It was just chicken stew.

"Enjoy it!"

Andy got back in his van. I waved as he drove away.

I wondered when he would finish his road trip. Originally designed to span the time between his first Burning Man and his second, it now seemed interminable. Maybe his cross-country driving was the same as his *Last Unicorn* quote: there would be no ending because nothing ends. As his planned "five to eight weeks, possibly more" on the road turned into two years and then continued beyond that, I grew concerned that his extreme sincerity would get him into trouble, that his belief in the inherent goodness of people and "the universe" was naïve.

I was secretly relieved when he found a young girlfriend—not the mer-maid—who hopped in the van, someone to share the journey. Though he'd been sharing it with tons of people—strangers and friends—all along, I wanted him to find love again. I met her when we were in San Francisco at the same time and they came to a reading I was giving in the fall of 2014, a year after Andy's first visit to Santa Cruz. He'd just been to his second Burning Man. Andy, energetic as always and dressed for Haight-Ashbury in his furry vest and cowboy hat, congratulated me. His girlfriend and I shared a warm hug. By then he called himself Magician and his girlfriend was Bunny. She was petite and cute and looked as if he could pull her out of his hat.

"We'll come through Santa Cruz on our way back to Reno," Andy said. "Can we crash at your place for a couple of nights?"

I was so eager to ask him all the questions I had: How much longer did he plan to spend on the road? Where was the documentary? What was he thinking, what had he learned?

"It's going to have to wait," Andy said on the phone a few days later. "We stayed with some hippies who gave us scabies."

He was humiliated about it. "Oh, Andy, it's no big deal," I tried to reassure him. "Come by after."

But he was already headed back East, toward New York. Next time, he said. I was six weeks pregnant, not yet telling people outside the immediate family, but I thought about how "next time" he'd most likely be meeting my baby, too. Andy loved kids. All his friends' kids called him Uncle Andy. One of the things he said when we broke up, besides that he was meant to love all people equally rather than one person especially, was that he realized he wasn't meant to have kids of his own, but to be Uncle Andy to all his friends' kids.

WE ONLY SPOKE in a few brief online exchanges after that. I saw he'd moved into a Bushwick loft, my complaint-turned-inside-joke manifested. There, he would take a pause from the road for spring and part of summer before setting back out on the road to attend his third Burning Man in August.

Within days of settling back in Brooklyn, Andy posted from the hospital. He'd woken up dizzy and unbalanced and was admitted. After legions of tests—and accompanying Facebook photos of vials of his spinal fluid, x-rays of his heart, MRIs—they found five lesions on his brain and diagnosed a sudden stroke at thirty-seven. I thought again of Greg and the swami from "The Last Hippie": enlightenment vs. brain disease. I'd felt something was different about Andy's brain, but I couldn't have imagined it was this serious. Had the brain lesions changed him, made him more reckless? Or had adopting a more "out there" lifestyle aggravated the preexisting but quiet condition of his brain?

I wrote him a get-well-soon message. I didn't know what else to say.

"I found out you were pregnant via a Facebook photo," he wrote when I heard from him next, a few weeks later. "How appropriate, and how wonderful. I love you. And by the way, your mother was RIGHT. I'm not 'him' for you, but I'm so happy for the lessons we learned from each other so you could be ready to meet 'him' and I could be ready for all 'this,' right now. I would never have been ready for my current life without that time with you. I'll come visit after this year's Burning Man.

I cannot wait to meet the new game-player you two created a time-and-space machine for."

I was concerned about him going back to Burning Man so soon after having a stroke. Wouldn't it be dangerous out there in the desert, with the heat and risk of dehydration, not to mention the drinking, partying, and drugs that went with the territory? I worried as if I was my mother. Then I reeled it in. It wasn't my place to comment on that. I was just glad Andy was okay and that he was coming to Santa Cruz to meet the baby. I missed his enormous personality and eccentric ways. I enjoyed seeing him in these little bursts when he blasted through town on his way to his next adventure. This time, I would ask him about his lifestyle, his goals, and his plans.

I still often wondered, *Why are you doing this?* But I imagined how Andy's story would play out. The narrative in my mind was convincing: He would finish his documentary eventually and end his road trip. The film would be good, win some awards, get him where he so wanted to be. I imagined him making it through Dragon's Gate to the successful directing career he dreamed of, settling in Los Angeles with Bunny or a mermaid or whomever he was meant to be with. We would visit with our families in middle age, and Andy would regale the teenage kids with stories of that brief time he'd spent as a nomadic hippie hobo on the road, and how much that short-by-comparison period had taught him.

In August, strolling around downtown Santa Cruz, I passed a costume shop with a sign out front: EIGHTEEN DAYS UNTIL BURNING MAN.

Which translated to: *Andy's coming here soon!* He'd return to our home and meet the owner of the time-and-space machine Jason and I had created, a funny, curious little chunk. I knew that as our baby grew up she would enjoy Uncle Andy's traditional post–Burning Man visits. Would she think it was strange that Uncle Andy was Mommy's ex-boyfriend? We could teach her that just because it didn't work out, didn't mean you had to sign off from that person's life, that Grandma Profiler had been both right and wrong about him at the same time: he hadn't been the one, but he had been the one for that time, and yes he had, as reluctant as I may have been to admit it, helped me "heal."

Late in the afternoon on August 15, a text came in from a friend in New York. I checked Facebook for the first time that day. It was already a mess of tributes and shocked friends.

"Andy died," I said to Jason.

I was alarmed by the flatness of my voice. The car felt cold despite the postpartum heat-flash hormones. I stared at the cars flying by on the freeway.

He never made it to his third Burning Man.

Tribute pages sprung up with hundreds of members, all posting their Andy pictures, stories, and memories. Then came photos of tribute tattoos—gold stars, shooting stars, and the saying Embrace Your Awesome in Andy's handwriting. There were even a few of a cartoonish drawing Andy had made of his face, which he sometimes used as a signature. I remembered something Andy had once said, that people often told him he'd make a great cult leader. There was, in his death, a cult of Andy. I saw how far his reach had spread and how many people he'd compelled as his Army of Awesome banded together in grief. Some promised to finish his documentary. (I can't wait to see it.) "He can change your life," another wrote. Every time an Andy friend saw the word "awesome" or the image of a star they posted a photo and tagged him. Others made a figurine of him that they sent around and took on trips abroad. Figurine-Andy had been to Italy, Ireland, Greece. He continues to travel. A music venue in Brooklyn dedicated a bathroom to him.

"An ad guy," I remembered he called himself the night we met at the reunion. He'd successfully branded himself, yet his brand was his own sincerity. He showed people they could leave cubicles and live their dreams. Many of the posts were along the lines of "the flame that burns twice as bright burns half as long."

As for why it happened, no reason seemed sufficient. "Can you die of sincerity?" one friend mused. No cause was officially given, so some speculated suicide. But I knew it wasn't. He'd never have killed himself before Burning Man. Others thought he'd known all along that he would die young, and the journey was a "bucket list" endeavor. This theory I also disbelieved. He was afraid of having Alzheimer's as he aged. I didn't think he knew he was going to die, but did some part of him know? Were what seemed like allusions to death just road trip talk? "Water flows and water falls," he wrote. "Down isn't always a bad direction." And: "If there ever comes a time when you are wistful in remembrance of me or a time we had together, don't let it make you sad. Simply realize that the wind doesn't go down. It's just an illusion caused by the world spinnin' round." I thought he'd made it up, but it's a misquote of— and more interesting improvement on—a Flaming Lips song lyric. He'd called himself a magician and he'd gone and pulled the ultimate disappearing act. It was a private death for a man whose life was constantly on public display.

In her essay "On Nostalgia," Elizabeth Evitts Dickinson writes of self-mythologizing on social media, "We want to make real this staged portrait of self . . . We are as obsessed with nostalgia as the Victorians were with death." Death alters our perception of a person, and the death of another affects the way we look at our own lives, at least for a while. At least until the waves of shock and grief go down, a shifting of the tides as we return to living without constant awareness of the brief and temporary nature of all this.

What I'd seen as Andy's brand of fortune cookie wisdom, dismissible as New Age, "Burning Man went to his head" joke fodder or entertainment, took on a new gravitas. I'd thought Andy's road trip needed to be ended—*Where is the end point, where is this going?* I often wondered while perusing his many posts. I'd thought the answer would provide justification for his giving up everything to do it. But he was right. The road trip was only for its own sake. Andy would have appreciated the way it all looked now that he wasn't here to see it. I wished he'd lived to continue his journey until some endpoint when he would have been satisfied, maybe even emerged transformed. I wanted to know what he would have done with what he'd gained and how he'd changed. Instead it stopped abruptly. There was no end. It became a different myth, a never-ending story.

He'd embodied the phrase "larger than life." Was he? Had he traversed the Dragon's Gate falls, been turned from a koi into a dragon, death having brought him to some next-level place beyond ordinary perception? Or was he one of those koi who'd succumbed to the perils along the way? I thought of how he'd said he had bad luck. But then he'd also posted a fortune from a fortune cookie soon before he passed that read, "Your pain is the breaking of the shell that encloses your understanding." And his constant quoting of, "There are no happy endings because nothing ends"—was this, too, fortune cookie wisdom, or was he more in touch with a mythological realm? Either way, mythologizing the self is supposedly a healthy behavior. In an article in *Psychology Today* entitled "On the value of mythologizing yourself," Tad Waddington writes that an "advantage of mythologizing your actions and of giving them a heroic quality can be seen in the work of the religion scholar Mircea Eliade. He observed that for people to have meaningful lives they must put their lives into a narrative, a story, a myth."

If Andy had achieved one thing, it was this. I was left with the question of why it had taken his death for me to finally understand his message—a message his death both undermined (the universe is looking out for you) and cemented (appreciate all the moments of this fleeing life).

In his article "To Be Happier, Start Thinking More About Your Death," Arthur C. Brooks describes how Buddhist monks contemplate photos of corpses in various states of decay. "This body, too," students are taught to say about their own unavoidable fates. Yet every day we ignore death. "'Am I making the right use of my scarce and precious life?' it makes us ask . . . Our days tend to be an exercise in distraction. We think about the past and future more than the present. We are mentally in one place and physically in another. We mindlessly blow the present moment on low-value activities." It's what Andy was traveling the country essentially preaching. Even now, he reminds me, *This will all be over in an instant.*

If I ever forget again, I know where to find him. I scroll to that image of his van, off-season on the playa, stuck in the mud. A memento mori reminding me that even stuck you can still make something beautiful. I'd made light of his fortune cookie messages, but as the photo that remains his banner on Facebook reads, "One must dare to be himself, no matter how frightening or strange that self may prove to be." It's one of the truest things I've come to believe. It's from a fortune cookie.

It's from Andy.

"Better to have it and not need it than need it and not have it," I remind myself constantly, lugging everything required to leave the house with a baby. Keys? Already clipped to my belt loop. Thanks, friend.

> The fear of death follows from the fear of life.
> One who lives life fully is prepared to die at any time.
>
> **—Mark Twain**

CRAB LEGS IN
HER CARRY-ON

M Y MOTHER SPENT her entire twenty-six-year career avoiding "hardship posts"—the Foreign Service term for places in which you could be stationed that might turn into a war zone. Every Foreign Service officer got one at some point. She dodged the seeming requirement. Until now. In retirement, she's immersed in her most challenging case. The initial few months she thought she'd spend taking care of my grandmother have morphed into five years and counting.

"After all those years, you got your hardship post," I tell her.

No matter where she's "stationed," she'll always be The Profiler. As a married, pregnant, home-owning author and college teacher, I no longer require her services, yet still she isn't done with her number one mission. With my love life off the table, she micromomages everything else. She's ever coming up with new ways to channel her Profiler energy. One of her favorites, still, is imploring me to GO FOR THE BIG SUCCESS!—sell a screenplay, write a bestseller—as if this were something one held any semblance of control over.

"If that kind of ideal 'success' were something you could purpose-fully make happen," I say, "Everyone would do it. What about you? You've always been a frustrated writer, you've had an interesting life—why don't you write a Foreign Service memoir?"

"I'm just saying, you could try harder. Does living in Santa Cruz make you less motivated?"

"No, the opposite. It's like a permanent writing residency."

"Then shouldn't you have a bestseller yet?"

And so the cycle goes.

IN SEATTLE, MY mother keeps herself entertained doing things like renting a metal detector to go search for treasure down by the lake, taking cruises to Antarctica and Fiji, and finding a drawing by a famous artist, worth $18,000, at an estate sale for twenty bucks.

When not traveling to far-flung locations or taking care of my grandmother, The Profiler comes to visit Jason and me in Santa Cruz. When not dispensing career advice, she likes to "help." Often this can be truly helpful—walking Baxter, pruning trees, fixing a meal. But it comes at a price: she'll give instructions on how she did what she did and further instruct us to do it better next time. Sometimes she sounds like an automated system that dispenses suggestions: "Your house is dirty, you should hire a cleaner." "Jason needs to shovel Señor Bacon's area." "Your neighbor tells me you sometimes forget to take out the trash on garbage night." "There's nothing in the refrigerator, are you eating out all the time?" "Do you know how your IRA is doing at Schwab?" She trimmed the tree on our back deck and in the process cut up a string of outdoor lights wound through its branches. When she "weeded" around the house she ripped out our favorite bush.

During my pregnancy, or because of my pregnancy, this all feels amplified times a million.

I'd been taking the birth classes and the yoga classes and know a calm emotional state is important if one hopes for a smooth natural birth. (Though sometimes the emotional state of the Buddha can't guarantee that.) My mother is appalled that I possess the desire to give birth without an epidural. She suggests I get it so that I don't have to "be a hero." There is nothing triumphant about birthing without pain medication, she tells me.

"It's not that," I respond. "If I need it I'll get it, but if I can do it without it that's an experience I'd like to have. I'd like to really feel it, to know childbirth in that way."

This is clearly said by someone who has not experienced childbirth, but in Santa Cruz I've met all kinds of people who'd done it drug-free— not just hippies and wind goddess types, but practical, down-to-earth women, too—so why not? Not winning the argument, my mother changes the subject.

"I've been getting these Alaskan king crab legs at the grocery store for Grandma and me. They're delicious dipped in melted butter with lemon. I'll get some before I come down there and bring them for us to enjoy together."

She still loves to micromomage, whether it's finding a man, birthing a baby, or what to eat for dinner.

"First of all, why would you bring crab legs to a city on the Pacific Ocean that has all the seafood, and second of all, how would you even bring the crab legs down here?"

"I'll pack them in my carry-on, between bags of ice."

"MY MOTHER WANTS to bring crab legs in her carry-on," I tell Jason.

"Why?" he asks. "And won't they get gross on the plane?"

"Whether it's a man or a crustacean, she still has to find the very best thing."

"Does she know we have a Whole Foods here?"

"I told her. But she wants us to try these special ones . . . maybe since the flight from Alaska to Seattle is shorter than to California, she thinks they're fresher?"

"They won't be when she gets them off the plane . . ."

TO OUR RELIEF, when picking her up at the San Jose airport, we learn she has not brought the crab legs.

"I thought about it and you were right. They might start to smell on the plane."

THE PROFILER IS trying to predict exactly when the baby will be born so she can pick out dates to fly down accordingly. I try to convince her to wait until the baby—who now has a name, Olivia—arrives. "Term" is anywhere from thirty-seven to forty-two weeks, so who can really say?

"Olivia will be born on the twelfth or thirteenth," she decides, adding four or five days to the midwife's estimate. "I'll come down on the tenth."

"I HOPE OLIVIA'S born today," I say to Jason every day as her arrival approaches. My "due date" of June 8 comes and goes with no sign of labor. I'm not even uncomfortable at the size of, if not a house, a New York City studio apartment, but I am convinced that having the baby out before my mother's arrival is the difference between a smooth or stressful process.

"If she's here, my cervix will tie up in a bow," I joke to Jason and our doula, only I'm not entirely sure I'm joking.

MY IDEA ABOUT kids was that having them would be contingent on meeting the right man to be their father. Then I got what I wished for. Jason's ideal family was us plus one daughter. He's so great with kids I couldn't imagine him *not* being a father. When he went home after our first kiss in New York, when we weren't yet dating and couldn't have known what was to come, he told his mother, "I met the mother of my children." Having children went from vague future possibility to something that could be really real, very soon.

I was terrified.

What if I wasn't ready?

What if I was terrible at it?

What if I lost my self and was never the same?

What if I turned absurd and one day offered to bring her some special shrimp in my satchel?

Even though I'd been so into the idea of fearlessness in the pursuit of my goals, and despite the situation I'd fortunately stumbled into, ideal conditions for becoming a mother in the way I'd imagined, I was suddenly very, very afraid of getting exactly what I wanted.

AT THIRTY-FIVE, I thought, it would take a while. Instead, I got pregnant in a matter of weeks. When we found out the baby would be a girl, The

Profiler was certain she'd be vindicated. "You'll see how it is when you have a daughter . . . how you'll worry when she tells you she's going to a friend's house and really goes out dancing in San Francisco."

"I don't think that'll be for a while, Mom. And anyway, she wouldn't have to lie about it, because I wouldn't mind."

BY THE END, I look Zen-like and composed on the outside—floating between prenatal yoga and big lunches and walks on the seaside cliffs of Santa Cruz—but internally I'm a wreck. My mother spent her first week waiting for the baby at a bed-and-breakfast, but for the past week she's been staying with Jason and me. At the midwives' office they're threatening induction. I want to go into labor naturally because I've heard induced labor is significantly more painful and I'm still hoping not to have to do the drugs. I spent enough of my youth doing the drugs. I want to be fully present for my baby's birth, pain and blood and poop and the primal mammalian nature of it all, I want it. By the end I don't care what I look like. I'm bouncing on an exercise ball topless in the middle of the living room and turning my nipples to pulp with a breast pump because supposedly all the bouncing will encourage the baby to drop. The nipple stimulation (I cringe when birth professionals refer to it as "nipple stim") will trigger the hormones that bring on labor. I while away entire afternoons like this. Nothing happens.

My mother takes the dog on lots of walks, goes to the beach, does her gardening. Jason acts as a buffer. We walk around the neighborhood.

We go eat dinner at Pearl of the Ocean, a Malaysian restaurant, and ask for extra spicy. The food comes out so spicy my mother and Jason—both spice aficionados—can barely choke it down. I like spicy less than they do, and I'm shoveling forkfuls of fiery soy protein down my throat, hoping to induce labor. When we get home, I'm convinced it worked, only then I notice that Jason and my mother are also in labor. This is not labor. It's fire-butt.

The midwife suggests getting away for the weekend leading into my forty-first week of pregnancy. What I read between the lines is "get away from your mother," but probably that's not what she means. Jason and I hole up at a Buddhist resort outside of Santa Cruz that's equidistant to the hospital and our house, where we hike and swim and sleep in a yurt. Two more days pass. Still nothing. We return to the house. Another week goes by. I am, as they say in the birth world, "forty-one plus six."

We go out to eat with Jason's parents and The Profiler. It's Saturday again, and I am scheduled for induction the following day. I've finally conceded. This baby doesn't want to come. My body's refusing to go into labor. I'm sad about it, but there doesn't seem like another way out. "I'm worried she'll need a caesarean," I overhear my mother say to Jason's parents when she thinks I'm out of earshot. My whole body tenses. *I will need no such thing*, I reassure myself.

Afterward, Jason and I go to the movies. Maybe crying in the movie works, because something starts to happen. Cramps. They get stronger. I'm up throughout the night, bouncing on the exercise ball. In the morning I lose the mucous plug. I call the hospital. They tell me to still come in at five to see if I need the induction. Given the contractions, I'm certain I won't.

"I'm in labor!" I tell my mother when she wakes up.

"Good!" she replies, as excited as I am, and we hug. What have I been so worried about? Maybe I could have a baby right here on the living room floor, my mother in attendance and all.

Jason and I pack for the hospital and go on a hike through the redwoods. Late-afternoon light beams through the canopy of trees. It feels like the beginning of an acid trip. It is beautiful. Contractions are nothing like in the movies and not yet delivering a sensation I would name as pain.

After waiting so long, I believe, this is going to happen fast. So much of my life has been like that—nothing, followed by everything all at once. And yet, if there's one thing I should know: just because something starts out low risk, don't assume there won't be complications.

AT THE HOSPITAL that evening, the midwife tells me I'm too dilated for pharmaceutical induction. Our doula asks if we can go home. The midwife says sure, but I decide to stay: my mother's at the house, and this room is nice, there's a tub, and they've already inserted my IV port, which, more than the contractions, did hurt like a motherfucker. I'll later look back on this as ridiculous, that one needle in the back of my hand could prompt my decision and the chain of events that followed. But then I still think the baby will be here soon. I opt for a Foley catheter, a drug-free induction involving a balloon that goes up inside and puts pressure down to encourage stubborn cervixes to dilate to four centimeters.

Sunday night I'm in actual labor, now painful but still manageable. The doula, supreme queen of angels, gets up from her rocking chair every few minutes to massage my legs when a strong contraction jars me from a haze of semi-sleep.

This continues into Monday morning. The Foley falls out, meaning I'm at four centimeters. Six more to go and I'll be pushing. Feels doable. We walk and do lunges. Another midwife comes by and wants to break my water. It's in my "birth plan" not to do that, but she says if she does it the baby will be here by the end of her shift. She seems sure, so I say sure. Things really get dialed up then. They aren't asking, on my request, about my pain levels, but I'd label it now as having gone, suddenly, from four to ten-plus. More lunges. Walks outside along the curb, taking stairs two at a time. In and out of the tub and back in again. Anything our doula thinks will help this baby's short but long journey. I feel annoyed when Jason sleeps even though I know he needs to. He doesn't have the labor hormones. When he's awake he gets in the tub with me. Later the doula has us do a thing with a rocking chair and the exercise ball. Jason hugs me, I tell him I love him. I go back in the tub and come out again, and Monday is winding down. If the baby were coming by now, as she was "supposed to" after the water broke, I'd be managing, but I'm still at four when they check. I know I need something. My mother was right. I ask for Road Of Pharmaceutical Pain Management Stop One: a narcotic. The nurse administers it. It does nothing. I ask for the epidural. They tell me something about blood platelets and that I might not be able to have it. I get blood drawn and wait another hour, the longest hour of my life. I'm starting to panic. I never even wanted an epidural, and now they say I can't have it? All reassurance stops working. They return and tell me the blood platelet situation has resolved. I can have the epidural. I'm even more relieved when it works.

I exhale. I descend into a state of euphoric bliss. If this were a more typical labor the baby would have been here hours ago. That would have been all well and good, but under these circumstances yes, my mother was right, and I am so grateful for this needle in my spine-space delivering sweet, sweet relief from all that trying.

Then the rollercoaster approaches another drop.

They're trying Pitocin in my IV. The contractions are stronger, but Olivia isn't happy about it. She's going into distress. "This baby needs to come out," the midwife says. There is a conversation of which I have no memory. Next thing I know I'm signing a consent form for a caesarean section. It doesn't feel like me who's doing it. The me that feels like me has gone elsewhere. I am a body with a hand and a pen, signing this form. Resigned. I wanted to birth the baby naturally. Now all I want is to at least push her out, but it isn't happening. I can't feel anything and am bed-bound. Total surrender, not to my body but to other people. If I could undo it all and go back to coping with the pain I would, but hindsight and all, and that doesn't guarantee it would have worked anyway. Saturday night to Tuesday morning. Jason shows up beside me in scrubs. Then they cut through my abdomen to free the baby trapped inside. I'm amazed and freaked out in equal measure, never having had anesthesia before save some novocaine many years ago at the dentist.

"I'm trying to avoid the tattoo," the surgeon says. The nine-point lotus tattoo that Andy's roommate designed for me to cover up the ex-husband one.

"Forget the tattoo, just get the baby!" I hear the disembodied upper torso I've become yelling. I'm nauseated. The anesthesiologist adjusts some levels of some substances and it passes. I hear a cry and look up at Jason.

"The baby!" says my mouth. The nose breathes.

There she is. And there she goes. Someone's carrying a huge pink baby across the room. She's a big newborn, eight pounds and thirteen ounces, out of my narrow five-foot-two frame.

Speculation has it she got too big for my pelvis. Cephalopelvic disproportion, they say. Failure to progress, they say. Whatever the reason for the rollercoaster, Olivia Lumen The Tiny Human is here. It's instant love, the real kind. Feeling slowly returns to my legs. I wiggle my toes. My feet look like floaties. I'm in shock at what's been done to me.

In the bed in the recovery room, she latches on and gobbles up milk like she's been waiting ten months for it. *At least one thing about this is working*, I think, my body trembling in a state of postnatal hormones and shock. I'm doing well for a C-section, they say. Impressive my pain level is only a two, they say. The baby is beautiful, they say. Doing a great job, they say. It hasn't all hit me yet, not yet. My mind has not caught up to my body.

I am grateful for my life and Olivia's life, but I wonder if I'd decided differently at the stay-or-go-home juncture, if I'd had more time, if I hadn't had the water broken, if only, if only, if only. There's no way to know. I love the baby, am so happy about the baby, but have a hard time dealing with the fact that it didn't go—not even as planned . . . it didn't go, period. That I needed surgeons to cut into my womb to free Olivia. We were both so healthy—I try to figure out what happened, but there is no definite answer. I become obsessive about birth and caesarean birth, perusing every website, reading every possible article about things that can go wrong during labor. Love the baby, so happy about the baby—but grieve the natural birth I thought I could have. Instead I had surgery, and someone I haven't seen before or since plopped a baby beside my head while a doctor sewed up the absurd opening that had to be made because the preexisting channel for birthing didn't operate at sufficient speed.

"You brought life into the world," our doula says. "That's the thing that is beautiful. Doesn't matter how it happened."

She's right, but I'm still unsure how to reframe, especially given the body thing. Months later, I still feel a strange physical urge that I need to push something out. It's the most surreal physical sensation. It feels as if I missed a step, as if someone cut the final fifty pages out of a book and left the last, leaving a jump in the story I can't make sense of.

They say every woman learns a lesson from giving birth. I look for one about humility. About turning it over. Surrender. Acceptance.

I've heard I will feel totally different. Other than not being able to walk for the first time since I took my own first steps, I don't feel all that different. More like I've touched death on the way through, but that happens no matter how you birth, they say.

OLIVIA IS A peaceful baby, huge, round, and healthy. Jason starts calling her The Dumpling, which gets shortened to The Dumpler. I dislike the nickname—it reminds me of taking something to the dump, or taking a dump. We've always made funny voices and noises, but now it feels as if we have an appropriate outlet. One morning, I pick her up and sing, "It's The Doompler!"

And that's how Olivia thenceforth became known as The Doompler.

When The Profiler meets The Doompler, she tells her about all the trips they'll take together someday.

THE PROFILER VISITS again when The Doompler is four months old. It's December, and we take a walk on the cliffs. My mother worries that the baby is cold. She usually worries that the baby is cold. She repeats her worries until I snap—only I purposefully withhold the snap.

"Mom," I say. "We have come on this walk to have a good time. Look at this beautiful ocean. But you're anxious right now. This makes us not have a good time. So we need to go back to the car and go home."

My mother relents and continues walking on the cliff.

I realize that the unintended side effect of having a baby is learning how to better deal with my own mother: with patience, with empathy, with kindness in the face of behavior that makes me want to react in a way that is other than kind. The same way I'd treat Olivia.

Caring for an infant has taught me to better relate with my overbearing mother.

I was afraid I wasn't ready to be a mother, but I was totally ready. (Is the only way to know if you're meant to be a mother to become one?)

The next day, my mother comes to postnatal yoga with me and is tasked with holding and soothing babies in exchange for taking the class. I can see by the way she tenses up that she doesn't really want to hold the other people's babies. She's not a baby person. She doesn't have the cuddly-mamma vibe. She's more of a drill sergeant. That's why I wanted the doula instead at the birth. I didn't trust my mother to give the kind of support I'd need during labor. She loves in her own way—by worrying ("Not always," she insists). By wanting the best for us. By threatening to bring crab legs in her carry-on, because these are the best crab legs ever. Some things don't ever change, but the way we deal with them can. Instead of trying to change my mother's behavior, I alter my own reactions. During the same visit in which I will "learn how to deal" with her, I overhear her complaining to Jason's father about our messy house at a family holiday party. I go hide in the bathroom and cry. *She's so negative and judgmental. The whole profiling thing was just a convenient cover-up for that.*

When she's stressed because San Francisco traffic is making us late to a cocktail meet-up at the Cliff House, the baby squeals in her car seat, and my mother says, "I don't know how you think you're going to drive all the way to L.A. on vacation with her." Jason calmly replies, "That isn't helpful," and the longest period of silence I've ever heard from her ensues.

Jason and I resolve to have a chat with her while we're driving to the airport: if she continues these behaviors, she can't stay with us. But then the last few days she improves, and we don't mention it. I hug her goodbye in San Jose. "See you in February!" And off she goes. Between December and February she will go to Canada, Mexico, and England. Then she will come back here.

The Profiler and I are still on our very own brand of hamster wheel. Only I've gained a new perspective, thanks to getting older, Jason's behavior specialist tactics, and becoming a mother myself. The Profiler and I lead weirdly parallel lives these days in our respective laid-back, medium-sized West Coast cities. Caretaking, a challenging job, is the mutual territory in which we find ourselves connected. She takes care of her mother, and I take care of my baby. Our day-to-days are eerily similar.

"What are you up to?" I ask in our weekly phone call.

"Taking Grandma to a doctor's appointment . . . going to the grocery store . . . how about you?"

"Taking Olivia to a doctor's appointment. Going to the farmers market."

"It gets harder as she gets older."

"Mine, too."

"I just want to sleep through the night again." (Lately, my grandmother has been waking her up at odd hours with complaints of bites from invisible bugs.)

"Yep."

Tending to beings on opposite ends of their lifetimes, we carry out our quiet days. I encourage her to practice patience, kindness, and empathy with her own mother, who infuriates her, and she in turn sends me links to baby development classes and intellectually enriching activities to expose Olivia to. While I call her The Profiler, my grandmother calls my mother The Dictator.

"Yes," I'll agree. "Her will is very strong."

"But she takes care of everything," my grandmother says. "She does such a good job taking care of everything."

"That she does."

Still, I imagine, when my mother's hardship post is over, when she lives (part-time) in Santa Cruz, some Sundays we'll take the kids to the beach, set up umbrellas and chairs, split the *New York Times* while they run around on the shore. Here's the thing. That family I always wanted—the one Jason and I are building—I can't picture without her in it.

NOW THAT I have a daughter of my own, I wonder how I'll s'mother her in my own special way. I'm sure there will be something that annoys her most, akin to my mother's micromomaging of me. What exactly this will be remains to be seen, since my role right now remains limited to milk, safety, comfort, and play. We take Olivia along to capoeira almost daily. A few months after birth I could train again. Maybe the routine of attending capoeira will bug Olivia after a while. For now she watches the class from her playpen, eating cereal puffs and doing baby-ginga to the tones of the berimbau. It might be the thing I hope we'll do together that she loses interest in, favoring ballet or computer programming, but if so it won't be an issue. Capoeira won't be the thing.

Maybe "the thing" will be the inverse of what my mother did: I won't suggest enough.

"You knew he was a jerk this whole time?" she'll say. "Why didn't you tell me?"

"Making your own mistakes is crucial to your learning."[10]

"But you could have helped me avoid one," Olivia will counter, and I'll tell her the story of Grandma Profiler and me.

"I'm a profiler, it's what I do for a living," my mother always said, wanting my recognition of and respect for her accurate judgment, a defining skill for her. For years, she was met with an exasperated sigh or eye-roll instead.

One early morning in my friend Amber's yoga class, I'm holding *utthita trikkonasana*—extended triangle pose—and it hits me: it's not a triangle. Olivia and I are our own, separate mother-daughter duo. I try to liken "the thing" to a cornerstone of my own identity: *What about yourself would you most want your offspring to admire while they're more likely to harbor resistance?* I imagine future Olivia, having been

---

10 I believed this before I became a parent, but the parenting book I read during my early days as one, *Becoming the Parent You Want to Be*, reinforces it: "When we intervene, we can take the struggle—and the victory—away from our kids . . . try saying: 'I'm sure you'll be able to figure that out eventually. I've seen you learn a lot of things.'"

featured in a parenting story about raising an independent teenager with boundaries, lessons I'll probably have learned with Señor Bacon's aid.

"Stop writing about me!" my imagined teen Olivia says, still all rose cheeks and eyelashes. "So embarrassing!"

"But Doompler, I'm a writer. It's what I do for a living."

"Stop calling me *The Doompler, Mom!*"

All I really know for sure is that, somewhere between combat boots and Tod's, a moment will arrive in which I find my feet firmly planted in a version of my own mother's shoes.

Because I am a mother now.

And so the cycle goes.

A note from the desk of

THE PROFILER

ATTN: OLIVIA

Dear Olivia,

You're only sixteen months old. Play dates, not "real dates," await you for many years ahead.

But, at the right time, as you grow, take a look at the Profiler pointers in this book. They are helpful in choosing friends, too, not just when seeking a romantic partner. Learn to be intuitive and observant. Use your head together with your heart. Quickly size up those around you, to better understand and interact with them. Learn to adapt your approach and dialogue to the different personalities you meet. You'll more easily get what you want or need, and persuade others of your points of view. Here's a test: Try it on your mother. See if you can convince her you're right when she thinks otherwise.

The world awaits you, Olivia. Enjoy your life adventures! May you travel and live to the fullest, but safely, too. May you find much happiness, friends, successes—and love along the way. A writer like your mom, teacher like your dad, or diplomat, like me, whatever you choose, go after it! And may profiling skills help you along the way.

Love,
Your Grandma, The Profiler.

APPENDIX A:

THE PROFILER CHECKLIST

BY THE PROFILER

ARE YOU SEARCHING for Mr. or Ms. Right but finding lots of Wrongs? Avoid dubious dates and walk away from trouble. Say goodbye to heartaches and wasted time. How? Learn to form quick, accurate impressions within minutes of meeting someone new. Learn to profile.

FIRST, THE FAMOUS ADAGE: "KNOW THYSELF"

The deeper you delve inside your heart and mind, the better prepared you will be to recognize your ideal match. Ask yourself questions. Be truthful. What is important to you? What do you value? Career, hobbies, pets? Family and friends? Money and material objects? Are you religious? Politically active? Happier center stage or out of the limelight? A leader or a follower? Easily upset or easygoing? Sexual preferences?

THEN, IMAGINE YOUR PARTNER

What qualities are "musts" for your mate? Respectful, supportive, considerate. Shared values, common interests, ways of interacting and communicating. Everything from physical appearance and personality to morals and life vision. Don't worry if you can't come up with an exact portrait. Think about it and explore. Dating is trial and error, whether you believe in coincidence or destiny. Looking for casual relationships and not the "perfect one" yet? That's ok, but still choose "good matches." You'll have a better time and maybe make lasting friends.

WHY IS PROFILING USEFUL?

You're at a party, a bar, work, or an art gallery. You see an interesting person or are introduced to someone for the first time. Start to observe. Who is he/she? What are they communicating to you, verbally and nonverbally, with their gestures and their eyes? Is he lying or telling the truth? Is she really an artist or an attorney? Profiling enhances your perceptive powers. Observe, think, analyze, decide. Then jump in, or walk—run—away *tout de suite!*

With practice, if you learn to "get an initial take" on someone, you can better manage interactions with him/her, a helpful skill for all situations.

You've read about Liza's dating experiences. Lots of Mr. Wrongs. Avoid these "bad-date distractions," whether you meet people online or at a party, bar, or other venue. Look carefully and think about what you are seeing and hearing. Through keen perceptive powers, you can know whether he/she is right for you!

LET'S BEGIN PROFILING!

Ready, set—now what? First study your "subject" carefully. Get an overall impression. What he/she says verbally is important, of course. But what is he also telling you through his body language or nonverbal expressions? The way each of us moves, gestures, and stands communicates a wealth of information about our self-confidence and honesty. Watch out for red flags—particularly nonverbal signals that do not match up with what someone is actually saying to you.

TAKE A GOOD LOOK

APPEARANCE

Clothing, choice of colors, hairstyle, jewelry, tattoos—tidy or unkempt?

Outside the U.S., appearance can accurately reflect professional, economic, and social status. Bankers or lawyers were well dressed for visa interviews. Image reflecting profession. Even in casual clothes, Europeans and Latin Americans tend to wear chic brand names. Check the watch brand, too. Usually expensive. So, generally, a poorly dressed visa applicant was not the successful business executive he claimed to be.

Careful, though. In the U.S., appearances can be deceiving. What you wear is not who you are. Silicon Valley giants may opt for casual hoodies and jeans. Americans' intellectual, financial, and professional levels are not always on display sartorially. But take a look at their style, clothes, hair, jewelry, tattoos. Is the person arty/hip? Business attire? Dressed in J.Crew, Abercrombie, Armani, or Sears? Do they have piercings, dyed hair, a mohawk, etc.? Look and think. You can form some opinions.

But let's not judge on appearance alone.

TOUCH AND PERSONAL SPACE

Handshake—strong or limp; eye contact; personal space?

How nice to get a firm handshake, good eye contact, and a smile from the person you are meeting. These nonverbal cues usually indicate a confident, positive individual, at ease with him/herself and encountering new people—like you. Personal space varies: a foreigner might stand closer to you—but don't be put off, he/she is not threatening by invading your spatial comfort zone. Some cultures just do that. This initial contact bodes well. But keep profiling and see how conversation and body language mesh.

A TENTATIVE HANDSHAKE AND EVASIVE EYES? NONEXPRESSIVE OR TIGHTENING LIPS?

Body language of a shy or insecure person. Uncomfortable, unhappy, or nonplussed to meet you—maybe.

FACIAL EXPRESSIONS, EYE CONTACT, HEAD MOVEMENT

Smile or frown, animated or immobile? What is their face telling you about their personality or interest in you? Do they look at you directly, or are their eyes shifting away or downward, moving, blinking? Watch for contradictions: is he nodding "no" when telling you a "fact" about himself or a "true story"?

Visa applicants generally don't lie, but some invent stories trying to get a U.S. visa. During interviews, I listened to what they said verbally, while analyzing their physical expressions and movements for signs of contradictions. When conversations and body language matched up, trust, clarity, and rapport increased. But suspicious movements, darting eyes, unconsciously nodding heads, hands wringing nervously, and tightening lips were signs alerting consuls that applicants' stories didn't ring true. "Visa denied!"

You can reject a potential date, too, by being alert to their face and eyes as you talk. If they are telling you the truth and are interested in your conversation, their eyes should be focused on yours.

BODY LANGUAGE DURING CONVERSATION

You're seated at the bar or standing at a party or event talking to a new acquaintance. How is the conversation going? Hopefully, it's open and respectful, with your new friend encouraging continued communication. Is your interlocutor facing and focused on you? Is he/she really listening to what you are saying? That can be challenging in a noisy, busy, festive environment. But if he/she is interested, profiling can help you tell.

When people are engaged in talk, they listen with their eyes—looking directly at each other with interest to gauge the other's response and maintain the flow of conversation. They wait patiently for a response, showing respect and focusing on the other person. We may use simple gestures— pointing or touching gently to help communicate the message. If you are standing, gestures of affection may include touching your arm or lightly on your shoulder or back, if appropriate.

Obviously, someone with darting eyes, checking their phone or watch or glancing around the room, is not interested in what you are saying. Time to walk away? Could be. Also, if they touch you, watch out for the patronizing pat on the head or controlling arm grip. Commanding, belittling, or controlling personality?

If you sit down, continue to observe what the person is showing you with his/her body language.

POSTURE

Leaning forward or back, arms or legs crossed, slouching or sitting up straight?

Poor posture and hunched shoulders can mean a lack of confidence, energy, or ambition. They may reflect an introverted nature, uptightness, or poor self-image.

GESTURES

Are their hands/arms animated or motionless?

Simple gestures may add to conversation. Constant, wild gesturing could be cues indicating dramatic, center stage–type, attention-seeking personalities. Individuals from foreign cultures may use gestures more than Americans as routine expressions of communication. So gesturing may be indicative of an outgoing, animated, confident personality.

HEAD MOVEMENTS

Nodding yes or no, tilting when listening?

Head movements should match the storyline. A tilting head can show interest in the conversation and encouragement to continue. A nodding head can show they are listening and agree with you, or are encouraging you to continue to speak. But, again, watch for contradictions. If someone says: "I just closed a huge, multi-million-dollar business deal" or "I got divorced last year," their head should not be unconsciously moving back and forth signaling no.

LISTEN TO THEIR TONE OF VOICE

What they say, and how they say it. Listen carefully to pitch and loudness. Note, too, their manner of talking: how they pause or stress words. Do they speak clearly? A self-confident person doesn't mumble. Is their voice overly loud—are they seeking an audience other than you? Is their manner of speaking too emphatic or strong? Possibly an arrogant, self-centered person? Are they expressing sarcasm, anger, confidence, affection? Words themselves may not tell the whole story—listen carefully to how they are said to glean any less obvious meanings.

Profiling may seem challenging at first. But you'll be surprised to find you already know many techniques and automatically use them in everyday interactions. With this checklist, you can become even more aware of the infinite clues people unconsciously reveal during conversations. Who is that person talking to you? Intellectually, professionally, socially, economically? Improve your own positive communication techniques with profiling tips—to speak confidently, get ideas across, influence others, and build self-confidence. And, if you're looking for that special guy or girl, get out there, get going!

Best wishes to you, and good luck!

APPENDIX B:

THE SPECIAL ED BEHAVIOR MODIFICATION EXPERT'S MANUAL FOR GETTING CONTROLLING MOTHERS UNDER CONTROL: TECHNIQUES FOR MANAGING YOUR S'MOTHER

BY JASON

THE FIRST STEP in changing any behavior is to discover what the function of that behavior is. What does it look like your mom is trying to get out of you? A lot of times people will say complicated things like, "She likes it when I feel like this . . . She wants to demonstrate XYZ," but usually it's a lot simpler than that: she enjoys interacting with you and has a system where she does her weird controlling stuff—and you respond to it, so she gets a reaction out of you.

What you need to do, recognizing that what she wants is for you to pay attention and interact with her, is to use what is called "extinction." Basically "planned ignoring."

Whenever she starts engaging in an undesirable behavior, you need to extinguish the behavior. So what you do is the opposite of what she wants. Terminate the conversation—take away your attention.

Besides ignoring, though, you also need to have a positive replacement behavior. You're trying to get rid of the undesirable behavior, and to do that you need to replace it with a new desired behavior. When you're extinguishing (ignoring), you need to tell her, "Mom, if you want to talk to me, you need to do *this*, you need to talk to me like *this* about these subjects." And when she does, you give her what she wants.

If she has a great interaction with you where she's not doing her normal stuff, you just need to be very positive with her during that conversation. Pay a lot of attention to her, lavish her with praise: "That's so interesting, tell me more," etc. Over time, she'll associate the new behavior with getting what she wants, and she won't use the old behavior because it's not working anymore.

The key to it is to not just practice extinction alone. You *have* to teach a positive replacement behavior. If you want her to do something new, you have to teach a new behavior and then reward that behavior. It's the only way.

SO, IF YOUR controlling mother wants to talk to you about your marital status, if she does it in a way that's making you feel guilty about being single, such as "When are you going to meet a man," "When am I going to get those grandchildren," etc., you have to tell her, "I wish you would ask me, 'How's dating? Did you meet anyone nice?'" Put it in a positive way. And if she continues in the negative way, you hang up on her, until she starts asking in the positive way—then you talk to her for an hour.

- Be consistent with "denied access"—denying access to what she wants (in this case, interaction)—until you see the positive behavior. Denied access is a great motivator.

- Do it every time. When you're teaching a new behavior, if even one time you reward the negative behavior again, that's usually enough to make the negative behavior come back.

- Know that whenever you're trying to do extinction, the negative behavior you're trying to correct will get worse before it gets better. They'll think they need to do the behavior "harder" to get it to work. Stay consistent and don't give in, or you'll just end up teaching them they have to do the negative behavior more intensely to get what they want. That's the hardest part: when things get worse, people give in, so they never teach their kid (or mother) to stop the behavior, instead teaching them to do it more intensely. You can't give in.

· Reward the positive. Always. Way more than you think is necessary. No one ever got mad about getting too many gold stars.

SOURCES

Lundy Bancroft, *Why Does He Do That? Inside the Minds of Angry and Controlling Men* (New York: Penguin, 2003)

Arthur C. Brooks, "To Be Happier, Start Thinking More About Your Death," in *New York Times* (Jan 9, 2016)

Laura Davis and Janet Keyser, *Becoming The Parent You Want to Be: A Sourcebook of Strategies for the First Five Years* (New York: Harmony Books, 1997)

Sara Eckel, *It's Not You* (New York: TarcherPerigee, 2014)

Barbara Ehrenreich, *Living with a Wild God: A Nonbeliever's Search for the Truth About Everything* (New York: Twelve, 2015)

Matthew Hutson, *The 7 Laws of Magical Thinking: How Irrational Beliefs Keep Us Happy, Healthy, and Sane* (New York: Hudson Street Press, 2012)

Erica Jong, *Fear of Flying* (New York: Holt, Reinhardt, and Winston, 1973)

Oliver Sacks, "The Last Hippie," from *An Anthropologist on Mars* (New York: Alfred A. Knopf, 1995)

Kassi Underwood, *May Cause Love: An Unexpected Journey of Enlightenment After Abortion* (San Francisco: HarperOne, 2017)

Tennessee Williams, *The Rose Tattoo* (New York: Dramatists Play Service, 1998)

Kate Zambreno, *Heroines* (Los Angeles: Semiotext(e), 2012)

ACKNOWLEDGMENTS

THANK YOU JENNIFER Lyons, Dan Smetanka, Rolph Blythe, Megan Fishmann, Shannon Price, Bethany Onsgard, Francie Jones, Matthew Hoover, Joseph Goodale, Michael Cendejas, Melynda Fuller, Kassi Underwood, Emillio Mesa, Micah Perks, Elizabeth McKenzie, Karen Joy Fowler, Peggy Townsend, Amy Ettinger, Jill Wolfson, Susan Sherman, Kathleen Founds, Dan White, Melissa Sanders-Self, Jennifer Cacicio, JC Sevcik, Vicki Jones, Leslie Sharpe, Susan Shapiro, Daniel Jones, Sarah Greene, Penina Roth, Matthew Parker, Glenn Gordon, Sally Crane, The Thurber House, Cindy Spiegel, Alex Garinger, Jack Davis, Claire Miller, Namonin Maryounani. Thanks to my families Gennatiempo, Scheinman, and Warehouse. Thank you Shmu for everything and thank you, Olivia. Thanks to Emir, Josie, Jen, Michelle, and Shara for enduring friendship, and to the RdB Capoeira community for all of your support. Gratitude to the people who gave me these stories: Julian, Nathan, Half-Danish, Andy . . . and, of course, The Profiler.

LIZA MONROY is the author of *The Marriage Act: The Risk I Took to Keep My Best Friend in America . . . and What It Taught Us About Love* and *Mexican High*. Her essays and articles have appeared in the *New York Times*, *Los Angeles Times*, *Psychology Today*, *O* (*The Oprah Magazine*), *Marie Claire*, *Self*, and *Poets & Writers*. Her work has also been featured in various anthologies, including *Goodbye to All That: Writers on Loving and Leaving New York* and *One Big Happy Family*, edited by Rebecca Walker. Liza has taught writing at Columbia University, UCLA Extension, and UC Santa Cruz. She currently lives in Santa Cruz, California.